Narcissistic Abuse

Narcissistic Personality Disorder NPD
and Recovery From Emotional Abuse.
How Dealing With a Narcissist and
Healing From a Toxic Relationship
(Covert Narcissism, The Ultimate Guide)

Robert Mayer

information contained within this document, including, but not limited to, — errors, omissions, or inaccuracies.

Narcissistic Abuse

Tablets of Contents

Narcissistic Abuse

INTRODUCTION

Narcissistic abuse is one of the most insidious types of abuse that can occur. Not only does it not leave marks, but it also seeks to leave its victim in doubt, and those around the victim doubting as well. When dealing with a narcissist, you may find yourself feeling crazy, feeling as though you cannot trust your own perceptions of the world around you, because, at every turn, the narcissist will seek to contradict you.

Oftentimes, in situations involving narcissists, you will find the narcissist lashing out any time he or she is not the center of attention. True to the story of Narcissus, the namesake of narcissistic personality disorder, narcissists are obsessed with themselves to the point of it being a fault. They are so interested in themselves that they fail to recognize the harm they cause to others, and even when they do see the harm, they lack the ability to empathize with the other person, providing no incentive to avoid manipulating or harming other people.

When you find yourself dealing with a narcissist, you may find yourself withering away over time. Your own needs become irrelevant and unimportant, so long as you meet the needs of the narcissist. You recognize that the person you were initially attracted to have faded away, losing the charisma and kindness that had drawn you in, and has left behind a monster that only cares about selfishly meeting his own desire for love and attention, and will do anything it takes to ensure he receives it. You may find yourself doubting reality, believing the lies that the narcissist spins to keep you complacent, especially because those around you who do not receive the narcissist's abuse likely believe the lies.

Luckily for you, you do not have to continue in that relationship. You are not obligated to remain with a narcissist, and you can decide that you want to step back. As you read this book, you will learn how to recognize narcissists, their manipulative tactics, their preference in targets, how to handle a narcissist in a relationship, and all about narcissistic abuse and how to heal from it. Treat this book as your guide to navigating through the difficult world of life with a narcissist and use the information wisely. Good luck as you take your first steps into understanding narcissistic abuse. Life can, and will, get better if you put in the effort to separate yourself.

CHAPTER 1

Overview of Narcissistic Personality Disorder

Narcissistic personality disorder (NPD) is something that has grown trendy in recent days. If you voice any sort of sentiment that is even remotely considered vain, you might hear one of your friends jokingly tell you not to be such a narcissist. However, vanity alone is not harmful, nor does it make a narcissist. Vanity implies self-confidence; something that most narcissists lack, despite how they present themselves. True narcissists, especially the most insidious ones, are much harder to identify than just pointing to someone for doing something vain and calling them one. There are several traits that must be present. Understanding the intricacies of NPD will be one of your keys to arming and protecting yourself from the narcissist's toxic grip.

Diagnosing NPD

A narcissistic personality disorder is characterized by three primary traits: Lacking empathy, grandiosity, and a constant need for attention. These three traits combine to create the quintessential narcissist, though there are more specific criteria to diagnose the disorder. In order to warrant an official diagnosis of narcissistic personality disorder, the fifth edition of the Diagnostic and Statistical Manual of Mental Disorders (DSM-5) requires at least five of nine specific behaviors to be present pervasively. This means that the behaviors must happen in various situations repeatedly in order to be qualifying. Despite five being the diagnostic minimum, people exhibiting less than five of these narcissistic traits may still be toxic.

Grandiose Self-importance

Perhaps the most defining feature that people think of when they hear the word narcissist, grandiosity involves beliefs that one is better than he or she actually is. The narcissist thinks that he is the single most important person in his circle; no one does anything better or faster than he does. The narcissist does not feel the need to prove this, simply accepting it as a fact because he is himself. That is all the justification he feels is required, as in his mind, his own grandiosity is an inherent fact of life. He will always believe he is more important than you, even if you have proven to be the better one at a particular skill; he will vehemently deny your own success and assert his own importance.

Grandiosity comes with a certain level of perceived infallibility as well; not only is he superior to you in every way, the narcissist believes that he is never wrong and never at fault. He may even go so far as to believe he is invincible, acting in deranged, dangerous, and sometimes entirely insane ways because, in his mind, the logic makes sense. If he is perfection incarnate, then, of course, he can behave however he wants with no regard to consequences. After all, his perfection means he will never make a mistake, which means he can never be seen at fault. If something goes wrong, someone else will take the blame. Even when provided with irrefutable evidence that he is in the wrong, the narcissist will deny it so sincerely that those around him may begin to doubt their own perceptions of the situation.

This can look as innocent as denying that he is the problem at work, pushing the blame onto someone else in a way that seems plausible but is unable to be proven, or as unhinged as believing that he is entitled to a close friend or family member's home, bed, and even life, and feeling as though he is entirely justified in breaking into that home.

Preoccupied with Fantasies of Unlimited Successes or Power

Due to the superiority of the narcissist, he believes that, by default, he is also entitled to the success, power, intelligence, or even a significant other, that comes with superiority. He will obsess over these ideas, always wanting more and never satisfied with what he can get. It is a game for him to get the best he can because he believes he deserves the best. He deserves a perfect spouse, home, vacations, cars, and anything else he can possibly dream up because he is more superior to other people. Even if his obsessions are out of the realm of average for average people, he will fixate anyway, and never relent.

Despite the narcissist's own delusional beliefs, the world is not perfect. He is not perfect, nor will he ever be able to find the perfect person to spend his life with or the perfect house. Life does not always go according to plan, and that fact is the ultimate slight to the narcissist. Anything that does not meet his standards of unlimited success or power or perfection is deemed unworthy and either learn first-hand what a narcissistic rage is or is discarded in favor of something else that more closely meets his desires. No matter how much he may believe otherwise, the world is not perfect, and he is constantly inundated with the world proving him wrong. His beliefs are constantly challenged by the world, no matter how hard he tries to uphold them, and he is left unsatisfied because he never attains the perfection to which he feels entitled.

This sort of obsession over always getting the best thing possible explains why narcissists frequently begin to grow more demanding in relationships. As their partner grows comfortable, they begin demanding more, and will constantly insist that nothing you do is good enough. No matter how hard you try, however, you will never succeed in meeting their gold standard.

Belief of Uniqueness

The grandiose superiority that narcissists cling to so desperately tends to lead to narcissists believing that they are unique. Not only are they perfect and superior, but they are the only one to be that particular combination. They believe that, with their superiority and uniqueness, they are misunderstood by those around them. The narcissists often look at those around them and decide that the commoners can never understand what the narcissists are going through because they do not have the same sort of viewpoint as the narcissists. They cannot possibly understand the pressure of superiority if they have never had to be perfect and superior themselves. Because of this, they seek to reject those who they believe are beneath them, and the only associate with an elite few, chosen because they are believed to understand the narcissist's perspective.

This uniqueness also provides the narcissist with an excuse to ignore when people around her voice their disagreements or displeasure. If those around her are disagreeing, then they must not understand or see things as clearly, with the special clarity that the narcissist has by virtue of her perfect superiority, and that is a justification for their inferiority. The narcissist sees this as proof that the commoners are uneducated and beneath her, and therefore, their opinions are as meaningless as the child that cries for dessert before dinner. In the narcissist's mind, a judge would never take legal advice from a random cashier at the store, and because of that, the narcissist feels she has no reason to cater to it. When met with protest, the narcissist is quick to disregard others, telling them that they do not understand.

Along with only associating with certain people deemed superior, she will also make it a point to only associate with certain brands or retail locations, feeling as though anything that is common is beneath her. She believes that resorting to shopping with the commoners would ruin her uniqueness.

This uniqueness, paired with superiority and infallibility, justifies the narcissist in believing that she is an expert in everything. She may also even use her uniqueness as a weapon, claiming to be the innocent victim when backed into a corner. She will claim that she has it worse than everyone else and will constantly try one-upping others.

Entitled

Similar to delusions of grandeur, the narcissist believes he is entitled to anything he desires. He does not feel the need to justify that entitlement and simply decides that he deserves it. Instead of having to earn what he wants to like the average person, he assumes it will come to him naturally, handed to him. While other people earn what they have in their lives, such as jobs, money, power, and relationships, the narcissist believes that the best will simply fall into his lap because he is perfect and superior. He wants everything with none of the work.

An example of this would be a narcissist asking a woman he finds attractive on a date, expecting that she will agree without thinking about it. When she inevitably rejects him because she does not know him or is uninterested, he will immediately blame it on her, and make it sound as though he had been doing her a huge favor by showing any interest in her at all. When his expectations and entitlement were not fed, he lashed out in return.

Tendency to Exploit or Manipulate

Narcissists rely on manipulation to get what they want. Narcissists are able to speak so convincingly that they are able to convince people that they are literally going insane if they desire to, and that power is frequently used to exploit others in order to get what they want. Even their personalities that they present outwardly are a manipulation tactic designed to make them more appealing to the average person, and they should never be trusted. Narcissists are masters at keeping their manipulation and exploitation behind a thin wall of plausible deniability that allows them to protect themselves if anyone ever dares to call them out.

When they are called out, they will deny it vehemently and frequently deflect blame. He seeks to put the accuser on the defensive to protect him from being exposed.

Pervasive Lack of Empathy

As no one with a conscience or empathy could be as manipulative and cold as a narcissist, it should come as no surprise that those with NPD or exhibiting narcissistic traits also lack empathy in some capacity. Empathy was developed to help people cooperate in order to better the survival of humanity, and without it, narcissists have little reason to ensure that their families or other small social groups are cared for. Lacking empathy means that they do not recognize when they are crossing boundaries, and nor do they have that motivation to stop conflicts before they get worse.

The narcissist, lacking some or all empathy, does not care about how other people feel or whether he is hurting them. He may have a general idea of how the other person feels, but he will never actually feel for a hurt or wronged individual. Instead, he sees those situations as important stepping stones to better his own scenario. If he can take advantage of someone else's pain in order to get ahead, or even to derive some pleasure, he will do it without hesitation.

Envious or Believing that Others Envy Him or Her

Due to the entitlement the narcissist feels, she cannot help but feel envious when she sees someone in a situation she wishes she were in. If someone else is chosen over her for a promotion, she will likely avoid congratulating the person altogether, and May even begin to downplay the other's achievement, spinning things in a way that make it sound like she is much happier not being in any sort of leadership role. She will happily point out any pitfalls of the promotion, even though just days prior, she was vying for the role. She may even begin to convince herself that the other person is envious that she does not have the same responsibilities.

Haughty or Arrogant

Narcissists frequently have a haughty or arrogant personality. Due to their superiority complexes, they often act in ways that are disregarding of other people, leading them to come across as rude, haughty, and arrogant. They believe that anyone who is beneath them is undeserving of basic human decency, and because of that, those narcissist treats others poorly. After all, according to the narcissist, a waitress should have gone to school if she wanted to be treated with kindness.

Excessive Need for Constant Admiration

The last of the diagnostic traits for NPD is the excessive need to be admired. Narcissists thrive from attention, something that is often referred to as narcissistic supply. This narcissistic supply is all of the energy and attention absorbed by the narcissist and is the driving motivator for all of their behaviors. The narcissist will do anything to remain the center of attention, even if it is unconventional or frowned upon.

Causes of NPD

NPD can be quite shocking to someone who has never encountered such malevolent manipulation before. Those who have never faced the toxic beast of narcissism struggle to comprehend just how harmful being around a narcissist can be to one's wellbeing. Upon becoming acquainted with such monsters, frequently, people ask how they are created. Did the parents go wrong? Is there an imbalance somewhere? Many psychologists have attempted to explain NPD from a scientific perspective, but none are quite in agreement for what causes a person to become so irrevocably shattered.

Sigmund Freud

Perhaps the most well-known of the psychologists that will be discussed, Freud believed that narcissism, at least in part, is a natural part of the human personality. Narcissism, according to him, could be identified as primary and secondary. Primary narcissism encompassed a developing child's instinct for self-preservation and was deemed normal by the psychoanalyst. In primary narcissism, children directed their libido, or mental energy, inward. As a normal child develops, that libido begins being directed outward toward other people as well as the child develops relationships beyond the one with his or her parents.

Secondary narcissism, which would be in line with NPD, occurs when the libido of growing children never gets directed outward. Essentially, the narcissist is stunted in development, and all libido is directed inward, creating a potential and tendency for megalomania, also known as an obsession with domination. In normal relationships, both people engage in directing libido toward the other, making sure both people's need for libido is satisfied, whereas the narcissist never directs any outward. This also explains why, in relationships with a narcissist, the other person feels drained and as though he or she is not getting anything out of the relationship.

Otto Kernberg

In contrast to Freud, Kernberg believed that object-relations theory explained narcissism. This theory emphasizes that parents or other primary caregivers are objects, and the earliest interactions and relationships between the infant and caregiver create a personality. The voices you hear as an infant and young child from your caregiver define the voice you will use to speak to yourself, and that creates the foundations for future relationships.

Kernberg applied the object-relations theory to self-esteem.

He, like Freud, believed that some degree of narcissism is a normal part of development. He agreed that narcissism occurs when an individual invests libido inward. He went one step further than Freud, however, and stated that adults can have a level of healthy narcissism as well, which is created through healthy and positive object relations. That healthy relationship with caregivers at a young age built sturdy self-esteem, and that self-esteem and the superego allow the people to cope with the disconnect between who they are and the ideal self that the ego creates.

If healthy narcissism is created by a healthy object-relation, then it follows that unhealthy narcissism is created with a lack of a healthy object-relation. For those without a healthy superego, they become self-absorbed and struggle to differentiate between the ideal self and the true self. Their inner voice also never learned to praise them, causing the narcissist to feel the need to seek that praise elsewhere. Simply put, Kernberg's belief states that narcissistic tendencies are created by negative early object-relations. The narcissistic behavior of black-and-white thinking and grandiosity are defense mechanisms created to protect the narcissist from a repeat of those negative object-relations.

Heinz Kohut

Like Freud, Kohut believed narcissism involved libido being transferred to another object. However, in contrast to Freud's belief that narcissists direct all of their libido inwards, Kohut posits that instead of directing positive libido outwards, narcissists direct negative libido to others instead. Oftentimes, this negative libido transference occurs because the narcissist fails to differentiate between him- or her and the object, creating what Kohut referred to as the self-object.

The self-object is someone that allows the narcissist to maintain his or her sense of self. For children, this is frequently a parent, guardian, or another primary caregiver. This caregiver shapes the children's values and the children, in turn, mimic the caregivers to learn how to behave. Much like how narcissists mirror their targets, children mirror their caregivers, which results in praise. Normally, children grow up and discard the self-object as they naturally crave independence and individuality, but narcissists never developed their sense of self beyond the said self-object. Without developing beyond that need, they are doomed to act upon the childish impulses and behaviors we have come to expect from narcissists.

Treating NPD

NPD is notoriously difficult to treat, as treatment requires the narcissist to admit fault and reject the notion of superiority, and as discussed earlier, superiority and rejecting fault are two of the key facets to NPD. As a personality disorder, there are no known chemical imbalances in the brain, meaning there is no real medication that can treat the symptoms of NPD. The only real way to treat NPD, if the narcissist is willing and dedicated to the process, is through therapy.

Cognitive Behavioral Therapy for NPD

CBT is a form of psychotherapy in which a therapist guides an individual through the process of altering his or her thoughts, feelings, and behaviors by disrupting the feedback cycle that exists between the three. Our feelings influence our behaviors, which influence our thoughts, which influence our feelings. This never-ending cycle creates a constant loop into negative behaviors, in which the narcissist may think he is superior, which makes him feel superior, causing him to act in ways that reinforce his belief of superiority. The only way to end that cycle is to disrupt it somewhere with cognitive restructuring. CBT teaches the narcissist how to identify these action-feeling-behavior cycles and disrupt them in order to create better behaviors and alleviate some of the key narcissistic traits.

With the tools provided in CBT, the narcissist will likely begin by attempting to remove the belief that he is superior. With that belief replaced with something more realistic, such as he or she is equal to others, the narcissist should begin to internalize that feeling, and will later act in kind as well. This sort of cognitive restructuring, however, requires dedication, perseverance, and the narcissist's wholehearted desire to change his behavior. Without that dedication and desire to change, this therapy will be unproductive, or the narcissist will simply manipulate his or her way through it without really doing anything to change.

Psychodynamic Therapy for NPD

Like CBT, psychodynamic therapy is psychotherapy. This one focuses on the psychoanalysis of the narcissist's relationship and perceived place with the world. It involves plenty of natural, insightful conversation between the patient and therapist, with the therapist gently guiding the conversation to learn what the problematic thoughts and habits are. Unlike CBT, which seeks to override the thoughts, psychodynamic therapy seeks to increase self-awareness and self-esteem in hopes of eliminating the need for the narcissist to behave in narcissistic ways.

Psychodynamic therapy compares the client to a puzzle to make it easier to understand. Imagine that the narcissist is a puzzle that a child has pushed together haphazardly; all the pieces are there, but many of them have been forced to fit, and are not put in the right places. You can get the general gist of what the puzzle is supposed to resemble by looking at patterns and colors, but you do not see the true picture. The therapist in psychodynamic therapy seeks to guide the narcissist through deconstructing this puzzle to begin putting it back together correctly. Through the various talk therapy strategies, the narcissist should be guided to a whole identity with no need for the defense mechanisms NPD utilizes.

CHAPTER 2

Types of Narcissism

Though NPD is bunched together, there are three main ways narcissists present, with three very distinct patterns of behavior. Some narcissists are loud, rowdy, and unapologetically grandiose, true to the stereotypical narcissist. Others are much quieter and covert with their behaviors. Another subset altogether seems to exist solely to watch the world burn. Narcissism as a whole is generally toxic in some way or another to those around the narcissist, but they vary in how toxic they can be. This chapter will guide you through the defining features of the grandiose, vulnerable, and toxic narcissist.

The Grandiose Narcissist

This kind of narcissism is sometimes referred to as overt narcissism, and it consists of the stereotypical narcissist. If you are asked to identify or describe a narcissist, chances are, the kind of person you would describe is grandiose. These are the ones who wholeheartedly believe they are better than everyone else, and they will always act as such. They do not care what those around them think about them and hold the belief that anyone who does think badly about them is mistaken and their opinion is useless because of that.

These people genuinely have high self-esteem, even to the point of delusion. This self-esteem becomes the basis for the narcissist's belief that he is always right and superior. Even with the evidence in front of him saying otherwise, he will absolutely insist that he is right. Oftentimes, the grandiose narcissist is the product of a disjointed upbringing or a feeling of having things handed to him or her. He truly believes in his high self-esteem, even if it is unwarranted, oftentimes due to growing up in a setting that granted power or superiority. This could be someone who had some sort of natural talent that constantly put him at the top rank effortlessly, or it could be the result of growing up in a household that taught him that he was better than others. If he grew up hearing that he was better than others, special, unique, and given some sort of power, such as over a nanny or other domestic workers, he may internalize that voice and use it in all aspects of his life.

The grandiose narcissist will not hesitate to tell everyone every redeeming feature or success he has had if he thinks it may be admirable. He will gladly offer up the information about his most recent performance review at work or the grades on the latest midterm if he feels as though they reflect his superiority. Even if he has to embellish the situation to make him look good, he will not hesitate to do so. Oftentimes, this bragging also comes alongside putting down the listener's recent achievements in ways that bring the narcissist up a level.

In relationships, the grandiose narcissist does not care about his partner or his partner's opinion of him. The partner and anyone else with whom the narcissist forges a relationship is seen as a tool, and if he feels as though the tool has outlived its usefulness, he will not hesitate to toss it out and replace it with something he believes is better. If he still sees use in the relationship, he will do the absolute bare minimum to keep the partner around and willing to continue the relationship.

Grandiose narcissists are notorious for refusing to apologize. Even if there could be some benefit to apologizing, the grandiose narcissist will refuse, except for under very specific circumstances. To apologize is to admit fault and to admit inferiority, and he refuses to do so. The only time a grandiose narcissist is willing to apologize is when the person he has wronged in some way is superior.

Oftentimes, the grandiose narcissist engages in what is known as magical thinking, which essentially believes that whatever he thinks is true and that if he thinks it hard enough, he can make it happen. This is a sense of entitlement, and the narcissist wholeheartedly believes he deserves without effort.

Pairing this entitlement with his infallibility and superiority, he truly believes there is no way he could not possibly get what he wants. The idea of not getting it is entirely inconceivable to him.

Despite this magical thinking, grandiose narcissists are the most flexible of the types of narcissists. He will always act in ways that will manipulate the situation, and even if things may not entirely go according to plan initially, he has no qualms with manipulating to regain favor and control over the situation. If he is unable to regain control and get what he wants, he somehow manages to convince himself that not getting what he wanted is actually what he wanted all along.

The Vulnerable Narcissist

In contrast to grandiose narcissists, vulnerable narcissists frequently avoid detection. They are subtler, sometimes referred to as covert narcissists by other sources. Vulnerable narcissists are sensitive in general, especially to rejection, abandonment, and change, and due to their sensitivity, they often oscillate between feelings of superiority and inferiority, depending on their environment. During periods of inferiority, the vulnerable narcissist seeks validation from others in the form of narcissistic supply with the intention of boosting his or her ego.

Oftentimes, vulnerable narcissists are hiding low or nonexistent self-esteem. They often develop a victim persona with the sole purpose of earning sympathy and allowing for more manipulation of the situation around them. They always seek to make themselves innocent in all conflicts, preferring the victim role. The victim role either brings others running to the narcissist's rescue, feeding her ego, or causes her to be able to point blame and fault on other people, even if she did, in fact, cause the problem to begin with.

Despite the victim persona vulnerable narcissists well so well, hiding behind a meek and quiet demeanor, they are quick to explode when angered or challenged. The more vulnerable a narcissist is, the harsher they respond to any sort of direct challenge to her ego. She may first begin to use passive aggression, wording things just right in order to deny fault in the future, but if that does not work and she still does not get her way, she will resort to direct aggression.

Self-conscious, she constantly obsesses over her own appearances, attempting to overcompensate so other people will boost her ego, even if only temporarily. In contrast to grandiose narcissism, which is born from unrealistic expectations, vulnerable narcissism is typically the result of childhood trauma and poor relationships with early caregivers who were supposed to protect her. She uses narcissism as a way to shield from the feelings of worthlessness and being unlovable and craves the closeness and attachment to others that she may have been denied as a child.

Because she cares about appearances, the vulnerable narcissist will seek to build rapport with others in any way possible, if she values that particular relationship. She still lacks some degree of empathy, but she is willing to apologize when necessary and recognizes how her behaviors impact those around her. Despite being more in-tune with others' feelings, she will still only act in ways that benefit her. She will engage in good deeds, but only if someone is present to witness. She strives to be someone that everyone looks up to, but only wants to be that person when eyes are on her.

The Malignant Narcissist

Both vulnerable and grandiose narcissism essentially show the inverse of each other. One involves inflated self-esteem while the other involves a lack of stable self-esteem. Neither of these is particularly toxic if the narcissist is not actively going out of his way to harm others. However, one kind of narcissist loves to harm others, going out of his way to intentionally create this sort of toxicity. Malignant narcissists thrive on chaos, loving the act of causing pain anywhere they go and thriving on the reactions earned.

The malignant narcissist frequently combines NPD with tendencies of sadism and paranoia, both of which are hallmark features of antisocial personality disorder. This combination creates a monster who revels in pain while still desiring to be the center of attention at all times. Lacking empathy, he has no reason to stop what he is doing when people are being harmed. He craves attention, even if that attention is negative, and if wreaking havoc is the easiest way to get massive amounts of attention, then so be it.

When attention is removed from the malignant narcissist, he will likely stir up trouble in some way simply because then at least people are acknowledging him, even if it is negatively. Without the desire to be admired by others, he has no issues with being the heart of chaos. Along with his antisocial tendencies, the malignant narcissist blatantly disregards the law and other social norms. He will lie just because he can with no regard for the consequence, feeling as though the laws are irrelevant to him due to his own superiority complex. Sometimes, the malignant narcissist will even pick up violent tendencies, resorting to terroristic behaviors or becoming serial killers. By having the ability to harm others, the narcissist feels as though he affirms his own superiority and importance.

When not causing trouble, malignant narcissists frequently appear charming, using their manipulation skills and perfected mask of charisma in order to gain trust. They are also quick to seek out physical intimacy, though it is meaningless to the narcissist. They see the intimacy as a tool, recognizing that it will keep their newest target more interested in longer in maintaining the relationship, even with all of the bad parts. Intimacy also becomes a weapon, with the malignant narcissist withholding it whenever it suits him best. The malignant narcissist recognizes that, for the average person, intimacy is used to increase bonding and deepening the relationship.

As a natural manipulator, the malignant narcissist always seeks out anything he wants, with no qualms about manipulating other people to get it. Between his lack of empathy, his flagrant disregard for social conventions and laws, and his sense of entitlement and superiority, he creates a monster that is hardly recognizable as human. These people should be avoided, as sometimes, they hurt others just because they can, with no provocation and no reason.

CHAPTER 3

Narcissist by Gender

Among much of the psychology world, it is becoming more apparent that men and women exhibit different symptoms for the same diagnoses. Certain symptoms and tendencies are more common in one gender while the opposite may be true for the other. NPD is no exception to this: More often than not, men and women with NPD present differently. Keep in mind that men are diagnosed and present with NPD more frequently than women.

The Narcissistic Man

Oftentimes, narcissistic men are grandiose. They domineer, strive for power and ultimate success, and frequently are quite charismatic, drawing in other people with ease. His delusions of grandeur are typically much more prevalent than the women's, and he often acts like and believes that he is the best thing in his world and in the world of everyone else. He behaves as such, assuming that everyone else can see his glory and recognizes it for what it is: Proof that he is superior. True to typical grandiose narcissists, he does not care about other people's opinions but does desire some level of admiration and power over others. As someone who seeks out power, he has no qualms resorting to domination in order to gain control, even if it requires mind games and manipulation to achieve.

One of these manipulation tactics that are used almost exclusively by men is referred to as self-handicapping. When a man feels as though he is going to fail in a legitimate attempt to do something, he will fabricate a reason to fail, whether it is drinking to excess to induce illness before an interview, or volunteering to work the overnight shift the night before exams for the class he has struggled in all quarter. Recognizing that the failure is coming, he feels as though he needs some sort of reason to justify it. If he can point the blame at some sort of outside source, he feels as though he can lessen the blow to his own ego. Since he knows that failing on his own would hurt and be to admit fault with himself, being able to manipulate the situation in order to push the blame elsewhere allows him to say he would have passed if he had not had to work the night before, or he would have gotten the job if he had not had that pesky stomach flu that caused him to be running to the bathroom constantly throughout the day, and even multiple times during the interview.

In relationships with others, the narcissist values utility above all else; so long as someone is useful, a relationship can be justified. If there is no use that he can discern, the relationship is discarded. In order to be considered useful to the narcissist, someone must be a good source of narcissistic supply, have something desirable, or be in a position of power that the narcissist thinks could benefit him in some way in the future. When in a romantic relationship, narcissistic men are more likely to unabashedly cheat without feeling the need to cover their tracks too much, and when they do, they are frequently involved in multiple affairs, oftentimes at the same time. He sees women as a representation of domination, and he feels as though he must be in a position of power if so many women are vying for him at the same time. By being wanted and important to the women, he sees himself in a position of power with them, as he has direct control over whether they get what they want or not. He also is granted special access to the most vulnerable parts of a person, as when you love someone, you are trusting them and opening up to them. Narcissists love to be in that position of control, and the more women that desire the narcissist, the more powerful he feels.

Within marriages, narcissistic men often have very little interest in children. Children are an annoyance and inconvenience, as well as a drain for money. Money, to the narcissist, is a form of power, and if he is wasting that on a child, he will feel as though he is throwing that money away. Furthermore, children represent competition for what is most likely his primary source of narcissistic supply: His wife. Children are born dependent on their parents, and oftentimes, women take that role. Especially when breastfeeding, a mother feels that responsibility heavily, and if the father is not willing to take on responsibility, the mother is putting in round the clock hours to take care of her child. To the narcissistic man, this is a competition that he refuses to lose, and he may suggest things that will force a distance between mother and child, such as requesting to send the child to grandma's for the weekend or insisting on a child-free vacation before mother or child is ready. Occasionally, the narcissistic man is a vulnerable narcissist, and when this happens, he may legitimately take an interest in his children, seeing them as a viable option for future narcissistic supply.

When engaging with other men, narcissists tend to view them as competition. Instead of seeing the value in creating an illusion of friendship or camaraderie, the narcissistic man frequently defaults to surpassing his peers in any way possible. Instead of seeing useful allies, he sees rungs on a ladder that are to be climbed up.

The Narcissistic Woman

Narcissistic women are frequently vulnerable to narcissists. They are sensitive and constantly seek validation to her self-esteem from others around her. Instead of seeing those around her as inferior and therefore untrustworthy, she bases her entire worth upon how others see her, and if she feels as though others look down upon her, she will look down upon herself.

When it comes to manipulation, narcissistic women are more covert, preferring subtleties like playing the victim, and she may even frequently resort to using her body, knowing that she can use her physical appearance to manipulate others, especially men, into doing as she pleases. Recognizing that her body is perhaps one of her most useful assets, the narcissistic woman meticulously cares for her body, keeping it in as perfect a condition as possible and lathering on all of the make-up, hair products, and skincare she can just to keep it as perfect as possible. She is not afraid to present herself sexually if she thinks it will get her the result she seeks.

Along with her preoccupation with physical beauty, the narcissistic woman has a higher rate of developing an eating disorder when compared to narcissistic men. Since her body is of the utmost importance to her, especially in her younger years, and her penchant for perfection, she meticulously obsesses over every aspect of her appearance. Her standards of beauty reflect what she sees in the movies and magazines, no matter how unrealistic or unattainable these may be. She will desire to have the media's projection of what the perfect body type is, and she will do everything in her power to get that perfect body, even if it requires her to starve herself or engage in other disordered eating patterns that may leave her body unhealthier than ever.

The narcissistic woman is also much more likely to view aging as problematic and something to be feared and avoided. She knows that, no matter how much she may try, age will eventually take its toll on her body. The inevitable aging process is a large source of narcissistic injury for the woman, and she will likely begin to spiral into cycles of vulnerability-fueled rages as she grows self-conscious of her maturing body. When this happens and she feels she loses the sex appeal she may have relied on in her early adult years, her focus for narcissistic supply shifts from other adult men to her children.

The narcissistic mother typically sees her children as an extension of herself as little more than an arm or another body part. She does not recognize that her children are individuals with their own specific wants, feelings, or likes, and frequently superimposes her own on them. As perceived extensions of herself, she treats both the children's successes and failures as direct successes and failures on her part. Because of this, the narcissistic mother will often push her children hard wanting them to be as successful as possible, so they do not embarrass her. She will not hesitate to martyr herself to better her children's situation if there is an audience, and she will loudly announce her martyrdom to anyone who will listen, reveling in the respect and awe she earns when she tells the cashier all about how she woke up at 5:30 that morning in order to assure her children had the most nutritious, organic, homemade breakfast she could make for them before taking them to school.

While an attentive mother who pushes her children to succeed sounds like it would be beneficial to the children, it overlooks that the children's own wants are ignored. She will choose what extracurricular activities her children join, and she will force them to perform, even if they do not want to. If the children voice their displeasure, or if they fail to meet their mother's impossible standards, they are met with the narcissistic rage that the mother keeps hidden away. She often uses guilt trip tactics when she feels her children have slighted her, demanding to know why her children insist on hurting her so badly.

Unlike men, who focus primarily on power, women tend to focus more on social status symbols. The narcissistic woman is entirely content spending inordinate amounts of money to get the top of the line cell phone every time a new iteration is released, and she will buy new cars to make sure she always has the best. Even if attaining these top-of-the-line status symbols causes her to break the budget or even go into debt, she will do whatever she can to make sure she looks important and deserving of the first-class status she believes she deserves. She believes these status symbols alone are enough to signify that she deserves respect and authority from those around her, and she feels as though they justify that she is better than others as well.

Narcissistic women tend to agree that one partner is not enough to meet her desire for attention, but unlike men, she is likely to keep the affair discreet. She thrives off being seen as perfect, and that includes being the perfect wife to all around her. Rather than flaunt that she has multiple partners, she will try to hide it, and if her partner does discover her affair, she will either deny it or manipulate him into accepting the behavior. She will make herself just desirable enough to her partner to make it feel worthwhile to remain with her despite her transgressions, while simultaneously working to belittle and break down her partner emotionally, potentially saying that he or she is practically unlovable and that no one will ever want to be with a divorced partner. Her goal is to break down her partner so much that he will put up with her antics.

Unlike narcissistic men, who see little benefit in making friendships, even superficially, narcissistic women love to make friends. Of course, friends are subjective here: She will have no qualms about throwing her friends away if it benefits her. When the narcissistic woman does make friends, she often seeks out people who are perceived to be a higher class like she feels she is, but she will make sure she still feels as though she is superior. She wants to feel as though she is on a pedestal, and desires to be smarter, richer, or prettier than everyone around her. She refuses to associate with people who she believes make her inferior, as that would be the ultimate attack to her narcissistic ego.

CHAPTER 4

Narcissism in Relationships

Though narcissists have a reputation of being monsters incapable of relationships, they do not start out that way. Hiding behind a carefully sculpted persona that has been developed to draw in and disarm unsuspecting targets, the narcissist can be found in a wide range of relationships. Within these relationships, they frequently follow the same pattern of engaging in a manipulation tactic called love bombing, followed by demeaning and breaking down the other person, and ultimately, rejecting the relationship altogether once something else comes along that the narcissist believes is better suited to his or her needs.

Romantic Relationship with a Narcissist

Despite their inability to truly love anyone other than him or herself, narcissists are frequently found in romantic relationships. In the beginning, the narcissist may present himself as the perfect partner, and you may find yourself staring, in awe, believing he is too good to be true. He seems to be exactly what you have always wanted, and for good reason. Narcissists tend to reflect or mirror back exactly what they think the other person wants to see to be better or more desirable, which allows him easier access to the narcissistic supply he craves. You may see someone kind, caring, and a fantastic listener, but this stage is temporary. This is the stage in which the narcissist works to learn all about you in order to know exactly how to manipulate you later.

After learning about you, he will use it. If you have a hobby, he will take it up and say he has always been an avid fan. If you want someone sensitive, he will play the part. If you want a family man, he will brag all about how often he sees his family and how close they are. If you want children, he will love everything about them and describe how he loves to babysit his nieces and nephews. Anything is fair game here to the narcissist, and once he has attracted your attention, he begins to love bomb.

Simply put, love bombing is the act of showering the other party with gifts, compliments, affection, or anything else that may traditionally show love. These will happen often and with an intensity, you may have never experienced prior to the narcissist, and that intensity essentially addicts you to him. You associate him with warm feelings that came during the love bombing stage, progressing the relationship quicker than you would usually be comfortable with, and you will focus more of your time and energy on him. He will progress the relationship as quickly as possible, and you will find yourself feeling as though you are in a fairy-tale whirlwind romance. Unfortunately, the relationship *is* a fairy-tale, though the ending is not what you may expect.

This honeymoon stage is short-lived, and the longer your relationship continues, the more the narcissist's persona begins to slip away. You may see just a glimpse at first as he pushes to see how much you will tolerate without leaving, and it may happen as raging about someone else, or it may involve snapping at you or calling you names. After the fact, he will promise it will never happen again, though he will likely never apologize, and he hopes that you will give him another chance because you love him and he loves you. Oftentimes, the narcissist's victim, so blindsided by the sudden change in personality, does forgive the narcissist for the outburst, trying to excuse it as a one-time occurrence. It will happen again in the future, perhaps with slightly more intensity than before, and again, the narcissist's target will likely try to excuse it away. Over time, the mask eventually completely erodes, and you find yourself staring at someone you do not recognize staring back at you with the face of the person with whom you fell in love. The abuse and narcissistic behaviors may have been normalized for you over time, and you have found yourself in a relationship you never would have believed was acceptable. This relationship may involve physical violence intended to intimidate you into submission or may be entirely verbal or emotional. Despite this, oftentimes, the narcissist's victim finds him or herself staying in the relationship, unwilling to give it up because of the hope that that person who initially won him or her over might still be hidden in there somewhere.

Eventually, even if you put up with the narcissist's abuse, he will likely grow bored of you and discard you. You may have lost whatever was attractive about you before, such as power, money, or confidence, and he grows disinterested. He will either pick up a new form of narcissistic supply in the form of an affair or leave you for someone else. He desires the honeymoon period, where everything is fun and new, and as soon as that honeymoon period settles down and the toy is no longer shiny and new, the narcissist is ready to move on to someone else.

Friendship with a Narcissist

Similar to romantic relationships, narcissists begin friendships with a whirlwind honeymoon period. Something about you has caught the narcissist's eye, and she seeks you out to add to her collection of supply sources. She will do everything she can possibly do in order to win you over and attract your interest as well. She may use her own standing socially to impress you, pulling favors with people she thinks may interest you, such as charming a friend to put in a reservation to a restaurant you mentioned that you wanted to try, though it is booked for the foreseeable future. She wants to make you feel as though she is useful and desirable and wants the praise that comes with being the savior that gives you what you thought was unattainable.

She, like a narcissistic romantic partner, will seek to mirror you in order to seem like you have more in common with her than you actually do. She will feign interest in your favorite things, even going so far as to research them to carry conversations with you just to impress you and make you like her more. As the friendship grows, you find it becoming all-consuming, drawing you from other people you would usually communicate with, and soon, you find her becoming your go-to friend for everything. You enjoy the air of confidence and charismatic nature that she has exuded, and you may feel as though you two are inseparable.

However, just like with the romantic partner, over time, you will notice her mask slipping further and further. Every time you try talking about something you have achieved or accomplished, she will somehow make it about herself. If you just got into a degree program you had been working tirelessly to be accepted into, she may congratulate you, but then twist it to be about herself. She may tell you how happy she was when she got into her program at the school that is better than the one you are going to, and that she had been so afraid that she would not live up to the prestigious school's standards, especially because she was helping her mother through cancer at the time, but she had done it and she was so proud. If you are getting married, she may suddenly announce that she is engaged or pregnant during her toast to you, drawing the attention of your big day toward her.

As your friendship grows, you will begin to see a pattern of her feeling as though she must constantly one-up you. If you get a new job, she will look for a job that is even higher up the hierarchy or that pays better. If you buy a new car because your old one was totaled in an accident, she will go out and buy a similar car with even better features, and then laugh about the coincidence. She feels as though she must be the best in her group, and her fragile ego cannot bear seeing other people have something better than her.

You will also notice that she is never there for you when you need her. Every time she has a problem, she expects you to drop everything to tend to her needs or help her, but if you are sick, injured, or grieving, she will not be there. She will somehow seem to drop off the face of the earth during your difficult time, and when she does eventually come crawling back into your life, she will make excuses for why she was gone that sound plausible at first until a pattern is developed. You will be placed in the position of having to choose between accepting that she will never be there for you when you need her or dropping the friendship altogether.

Working with a Narcissist

At work, you expect a certain standard of polite professionalism. You feel as though you should be free to work without fear of harassment or abuse, and most companies would agree you deserve that: There are entire departments in many larger companies dedicated solely to making sure you, as an employee, are treated fairly and free from abuse. Despite that human resources department, however, sometimes, narcissists manage to sneak through the cracks. True to their inherent desire to be the best and need to seek out power, these narcissists are frequently found in higher up jobs that entail power, such as supervisors or department managers.

It can be entirely draining to work under a narcissist, and if you have the misfortune of finding yourself employed by one, expect a certain degree of insensitivity. Lacking empathy and feeling as though he is superior anyway, he will not concern himself with the feelings of the employees, even if the feelings are rational and justified. If you dare ask for help, he likely expects you to figure out the problem yourself and not make waves. He may also try to shoulder off responsibilities onto you just to get out of them, and despite the extra work you find yourself putting in, he will deny you when you ask for a raise or may decide to schedule you during your vacation you have been planning for months. To the narcissistic employer, you are little more than a tool of the company, no different than one of the printers or computers, and expected to simply follow commands, no matter what without complaint. Anything short of perfect obedience is considered offensive and unacceptable.

Even though you may find yourself completing more than your fair share of the work, the narcissistic boss will likely try to lay claim to the credit, or may even decide to downplay what work you did put in. After all, admitting that you had done the job instead would take away her precious attention and would detract from the success. Even in cases where you are great at your job, the narcissistic boss will not praise you, and if your own successes begin to make the narcissist feel threatened, he will often throw extra challenges at you to try to hinder you, or conversely, order you to do something that he knows you will fail simply to cause the failure to mar your track record.

When working with a narcissistic boss, any time you may try to point out a mistake or say something that is perceived as a challenge, the narcissist will respond in anger. True to narcissistic nature, the boss cannot tolerate any sort of criticism, and he will find a way to make the situation spin around to be your fault, even if the logic is faulty at best.

Narcissistic Family Members

Narcissistic familial relationships are some of the most difficult to navigate through. After all, you often hear that family has to stick together, no matter what, and that family members are the only people that will unconditionally have your back. Oftentimes, we feel obligated to interact and continue relationships with narcissistic family members, and because that obligation is there, the narcissist will abuse it. The narcissist sees this blood bond as a shield that will enable her own narcissistic abuse to be tolerated far longer than anyone around her would tolerate it, especially in cases where the narcissist is a parent.

Narcissistic parents are typically inefficient and rarely create healthy children. If a child does grow into adulthood without too many scars, it is despite the parents, not because of them. Narcissistic parents typically are either incredibly controlling of the child, seeing him or her as little more than an extension, or negligent and uninterested in the child. Sometimes, the narcissistic parent is overall abusive in general, complete with physical and emotional abuse. Oftentimes, narcissistic mothers dote on their children and raise them with the expectation that they will be her perfect extensions as they navigate the world. Her children will be little more than extensions of her own body, and she will claim their home, property, or even successes as her own.

As the child grows and naturally seeks out independence, the narcissist's parenting methods double down: Lacking the empathy necessary to recognize her children's needs, she begins enforcing control more and more, quashing any signs that her child is seeking independence. She will point out when the child fails, focusing on it rather than nurturing and recognizing the successes, and she will do everything in her power to make the narcissist fall back in line, even if that requires cruelty or abuse.

When the narcissistic family member is not a parent, but rather a grandparent, aunt, uncle, or of other relations, they often seek to make the young child a source of narcissistic supply. Following the typical love-bombing stage, they will frequently shower young children with gifts while ignoring any children old enough to form and voice opinions. As the child ages, however, and begins to see the world for what it is and voices concerns or disagreements, the child is frequently discarded, especially if there is a younger child in the family. This can be incredibly harmful to young children, as they go from being showered in love and attention to suddenly being rejected and outcast.

When the child grows to adulthood, however, he or she is expected to cater to the narcissist's every whim in the name of the family, though anything did will never be good enough. This cycle is likely to repeat through generations if not stopped and can be incredibly harmful to young children's minds.

Co-Parenting with a Narcissistic Ex

Co-parenting is never easy, but with narcissists, it is an entirely different ball game. When relationships fail without children, the dissolution is usually relatively quick and permanent, but when children are involved, that relationship can never be fully dissolved. You can never fully disentangle yourself from your ex-partner if you have children with him or her, and because of that, even if you divorce or leave a narcissist, you may be forced to continue some degree of contact.

When co-parenting, no matter how much you would rather not, you will be required to offer your child to the narcissist if there is a court order dictating it. Because of that, the narcissist frequently uses the children as a tool to manipulate and hurt you. He knows that the children are the one link between the two of you, and he will not hesitate to throw them under the proverbial bus in order to hurt you the way you hurt him when you initiated the separation. He may suddenly refuse to take the children just because he knows you had plans during his parenting time and it is too late to get a sitter, or he may decide to take parenting time or phone calls during disruptive times. Ultimately, all he cares about is inflicting pain on you in any way possible.

Narcissists typically desire to look as desirable and admirable as possible, but they want to do that with the bare minimum effort. Even if he takes the children for his parenting time just because he knows you cannot bear being separated from them, he may neglect to do anything the children need, such as maintaining hygiene or preparing healthy food. He may also take the children just to hand them over to his family members, especially if you dislike certain ones because it saves him the hassle and he is uninterested in his children anyway.

You must be prepared to deal with the narcissist playing mind games with his children, as well. When in a conflict, he may stop giving any attention or affection to them, and he will always push the blame on you to make you look worse in your children's eyes. He will say that you said he could not do something, or that you made him so angry that he could not take them to the amusement park as he had promised. This tactic, known as parental alienation, is meant to drive a wedge between you and your children to hurt you.

With the above mentioned, you can see that narcissists are rarely effective at co-parenting. They care about themselves more than anything and will not do right by their children simply because that is what parents do. Every action will be self-serving, and without the ability to empathize with his children, he will never be effective at parenting either.

When stuck in a co-parenting relationship with a narcissist, the best thing you can do is to keep contact at a minimum and document everything. Do not talk badly about your child's other parent, and let the child make decisions on the narcissistic parent without your influence. The most important thing to remember when co-parenting with a narcissist is to support your child through this difficult process.

CHAPTER 5

Narcissist's Manipulative Techniques

Exploitative and lacking empathy, narcissists are masters at manipulating others. They frequently have several tactics they employ in order to manipulate their targets, and the most effective and common of the tactics will be provided in this chapter. Through reading these tactics, you will find yourself better prepared to recognize when a narcissist or other person is attempting to manipulate you. When armed with the knowledge, you will be able to step away from the mind games altogether in order to avoid falling into the narcissist's manipulative traps.

Mirroring

Perhaps one of the most important of the tactics employed by narcissists is mirroring. In this, the narcissist creates a persona that she believes will be desirable to others. This persona is created to hide behind that enables her to pretend to be someone she is not. After all, her true self as a narcissist would be largely undesirable to all and would mark her as a social pariah. Because of this, she seeks to create a persona.

This is done by reflecting or mirroring back the person the narcissist is trying to win over. This can be done through picking up mannerisms or quirks that the other person exhibits, or deciding that her favorite food, color, television drama, animal, and preference in music are the same as yours in order to make you seem more common. She sees you as being someone to envy, and because of that, she attempts to mimic as much about you as she can. She wants to be whatever it was within you that attracted her attention in the first place. While some degree of mirroring is normal in human behavior to create rapport between each other, narcissists take this to an entirely different level. The narcissist wants to make it seem like you and she has more in common. You will naturally be attracted to people with similar likes, interests, and preferences as yourself, so she aims to become the ultimate mirror to attract you.

The reason for this manipulative behavior is because narcissists fail to develop their own stable sense of self. Because they lack that sense of who they are and are so fragile and fractured, they seek to mirror others. If someone is attracted to the narcissist for some reason, he or she must be worth mirroring, and the narcissist does just that. They create their mirror image in hopes of earning what the other person has, and to fake a relationship. Since the narcissist lacks the capacity for empathy, the closest thing she can do is mirror the other person, essentially erasing her own self in favor of seeing the world as someone else.

Projecting

Projecting is essentially mirroring, but it works the other way around. Instead of pretending to be someone else, the narcissist projects himself onto the other person. Typically, the projection is something true about the narcissist that the narcissist is desperately trying to deny, so he instead projects that part of him onto other people. That allows him to live in denial that he is the problem and allows him the reality he believes.

These projections are typically either positive or negative, depending on the narrative the narcissist is trying to portray, and there is rarely anything in between. The narcissist is usually projecting some of his own behaviors or his feelings toward himself onto other people to cope with the feelings or behaviors. For example, consider a narcissist who accuses an employee of trying to steal credit for work he did when in reality, the narcissist has been stealing credit for ages. Likewise, if you are in a relationship with a narcissist and he has a tendency of engaging in demeaning or abusive behavior, he may be quick to call you abusive if you ever upset him.

This tactic has a particularly useful benefit to the narcissist:

When he projects negatively, he almost immediately puts the other person on the defensive, which detracts attention from his own transgressions. Because the other person suddenly feels the need to prove that the narcissist is wrong, attention is on the other person, and the narcissist is free to continue on his way, never changing his behaviors. This leaves the other person feeling as though he or she is walking on eggshells while focusing intently on proving the narcissist wrong.

This behavior is also often exhibited by narcissistic parents on their children. They project onto their children, creating either a scapegoat or a projection of a golden child. The scapegoat represents everything wrong with the narcissist and serves as an outlet for all of the self-loathing that narcissists frequently internalize. If the narcissist is sensitive about intelligence issues, he may insist that the scapegoat is stupid and incapable, no matter how smart the scapegoat may be in reality. In contrast, the golden child is everything the narcissist loves or wants to be. The golden child can do no wrong and is oftentimes spoiled and coddled. The golden child frequently feels pressure to obey the parents at all costs in fear of losing the golden status, while the scapegoat constantly vies for any scraps of affection or acknowledgment. The scapegoat never receives this, and ultimately spends time uselessly trying to better his or her parent's opinions. Both the scapegoat and the golden child are seen not as people, but as blank screens for the narcissist to project onto, and because of that, neither gets the opportunity to grow and flourish.

Playing the Victim

Especially for vulnerable narcissists, playing the victim is one of the most effective methods to manipulate others. Oftentimes, these narcissists will try to get something they want, and when denied, they turn things around to make themselves the victim. For example, if a narcissistic mother-in-law wants more access to grandchildren and you hesitate, she may cry to her own child that the grandchildren know their other grandmother so much better and say how much of a shame it is that they will never get the chance to know her before she dies. She may also point out how the grandchildren's other parent must clearly hate her for restricting access so much, and that if she is such a big burden, she will no longer bother trying to see the kids. Oh, and be sure to let them know how much she loves them and wishes she could see her grandchildren more.

This entire diatribe is spewed to make you sympathize with her and feel as though you have to give her what she wants to make her feel better. She words things in such a way that makes it appears she is the victim when in reality, the reason that she is restricted from the grandchildren is that she would not stop stomping over boundaries and lavishing the children in candy while telling them to keep secrets from their parents about things they did.

Love Bombing

Despite how pleasant love bombs may sound, they are quite manipulative. They seek to create a sort of addiction to the one showering you in affection. In many of the non-familial, non-workplace relationships with narcissists, love bombing is a frequent favorite tactic. Narcissists rely on this tactic in order to create and bolster feelings of love and attachment to them to manipulate their targets into being more receptive to abuse in the future. It is meant to make them look more desirable to the target and draw the target in closer. As the love bombing continues, the target craves contact with the narcissist, focusing on the good feelings earned when being showered with gifts.

These gifts could be anything, ranging from thoughtful little trinkets that show that the narcissist was listening to you when you were talking, too expensive, high-end items you feel wrong for accepting, especially so early into the relationship. He may invite you on exotic vacations or take you on cruises, and even if you resist initially, he will insist that you accept.

As time passes, the love bombing increases in frequency, and you may find yourself reflecting on the situation, trying to decide if the gifts are overbearing or thoughtful and romantic. He wants you to develop a close attachment to him, and these trinkets are nothing if they will award him your affection and loyalty.

Triangulating

As implied by the name, triangulation involves three different people. Typically, it is the narcissist in the middle of a situation with two others. When engaging in triangulation, the narcissist creates a conflict intentionally between the other two people. This usually involves giving each person a slightly different story that puts the other person at fault. This encourages conflict between the two other people and allows the narcissist to sit back and watch the chaos without any blame. As the two bicker and fight, they are too focused on each other to focus on what actually happened, and a wedge is forced between the two of them. This is especially useful when a narcissist needs to sever an alliance or friendship.

For example, imagine a case in which there is a friend group consisting of the narcissist that we will name Allie for easy reference, and a friend named Brittany, and a friend named Callie. Both Callie and Brittany have a crush on the same person, who we will call Dave, and each has confided this crush in Allie, though they have not told each other yet because they know the other person also likes Dave. Callie and Brittany are great friends and Allie is the new person in the friend group. One day, Callie is hanging out with Allie alone, and she makes mention that Brittany had told her that Callie is interested Dave, but Brittany wants him too and had planned on telling Callie that Dave hates how she looks so she would not try to pursue him. Immediately, Callie feels annoyed at the situation and she tries to keep her distance from Brittany because she feels hurt and betrayed. Meanwhile, Allie hangs out with Brittany, who casually mentions that Callie has been keeping her distance and that she hopes Callie is okay. Allie tells Brittany that Callie had been planning on telling Brittany that Dave does not like her or how she talks in hopes of deterring her from pursuing Dave.

This leaves both Brittany and Callie upset at each other and unwilling to speak about the situation. Because they are both so overwhelmed with their feelings of betrayal, neither think that they should stop and consider why the other would ever do such a thing, and they each hang out with Allie individually. Allie is happy because she no longer feels as though she needs to fight with another person to get her narcissistic supply.

Gaslighting

While all manipulation is wrong, gaslighting is especially heinous in its own way. Gaslighting involves convincing the other person that he or she is perceiving reality incorrectly, causing doubt in his or her sanity. The name for this type of manipulation comes from the play published in 1938 called *Gas Light*, which involved a man convincing his wife that the lights in their home are not dimming every time he goes to an area of the home that is blocked off and turns on the light. When she questions him about the lights dimming, he insists that they never did, and she begins to doubt her own sanity.

Narcissists employ this when they want to deny the existence or occurrence of something that they know would ruin them. For example, the narcissist will deny any claims that she had said something cruel, telling her target that in reality, he had said those cruel things to him. Over time, with plenty of unwavering insistence from the narcissist, the target begins to believe her. As soon as this begins and he starts to doubt his own perceptions, he becomes more easily manipulated, as all she has to do is remind him that he is wrong and things happened another way. Over time, he takes that as evidence that he is losing his sanity and trusts her at her word. He begins to doubt everything that happens and everything that he believes happened because he feels as though his own perceptions are no longer trustworthy, and he will default to whatever the narcissist says.

Intimidating

When all else fails, the narcissist will resort to intimidation. This can be physical or verbal and can range from veiled threats hidden behind plausible deniability, such as saying that you will not like what happens if you do not obey, to overt threats such as threatening to hurt you or take your children away if you do not stop and listen. He will use everything you told him in confidence to hurt you or threaten you into obedience, and may even resort to punching doors, throwing dishes at walls, or engaging in other risky and dangerous behavior to prove that he is deadly serious in hopes of scaring you into submission. He may even physically hurt you to teach you a lesson. He wants you to fear the consequences of disobeying or denying him what he desires, and like you are better off putting up with the narcissist's behaviors instead of attempting to leave because it is easier to stomach.

Insulting and Belittling

Similar to intimidating, narcissists will frequently insult, belittle, or demean anything that you do. Narcissists thrive on making other people miserable as it boosts their own egos, and he loves to validate his own existence and skills by making you doubt yours. He will often fling insults at you, and when you feel annoyed by it and call him out, he will laugh it off and tell you it was a joke that you should not take so seriously.

By laughing and claiming it was a joke and that you are being too sensitive, the narcissist is making you feel insecure. You feel bad for being offended and feel bad that the implication of being bad at something was enough to make you feel offended, leaving you striving to do better and more in hopes of pleasing the narcissist. For example, if the narcissist claims that you are awful at playing his favorite video game and that you are not good enough to play with him, even casually, you may seriously work toward becoming better at the game in order to win the acknowledgment that would come with learning to play better. Unfortunately, however, the narcissist is never satisfied, and no matter how hard you may try to please him, he will never be wholly satisfied with who you are. There will always be something else to insult, and even if there is nothing left, he will make something else up instead.

Lying and False Promises

Narcissists tend to lie if it suits them. If they do something that upsets you, they will lie and say they did not mean to hurt you and they will never do it again. These false promises keep you clinging to hope that the future will be better, when in reality; the narcissist has no interest in changing or bettering his behavior. So long as the narcissist was thorough enough in the love bombing stage, the target is so enamored with the idea of the person he was in the early stages that the target will overlook those transgressions. Unfortunately to the target, however, that persona was little more than an act and as soon as it was no longer needed to win over the person of choice, that persona was discarded.

The narcissist may apologize and attempt to do better if you make it clear that you are done with the abuse and mistreatment and that you are leaning toward ending the relationship altogether. His promise might not mean much, but when you see him bringing back that person you fell in love with, you may be more willing to overlook it. You want to believe that the narcissist is a good person and can change.

Unfortunately, that change is only temporary and will not last. Because the narcissist lacks empathy and does not see how it could possibly benefit him, he sees no reason to go beyond the bare minimum to keep you interested in him.

FOG (Fear, Obligation, Guilt)

Narcissists frequently let their victims get lost in the FOG in the relationship. Just like how in real fog, it is impossible to see or navigate safely or effectively, navigating the FOG is incredibly difficult. When lost in FOG, you struggle to see that some of the behaviors are dangerous or unhealthy, and your ability to evaluate your relationship is clouded and obscured. FOG stands for fear, obligation, and guilt, and narcissists love getting their victims stuck and lost in it.

When you are afraid of a relationship or situation, you are much more likely to be obedient simply due to self-preservation. Narcissists know that and they want you to be afraid. Fear is a response to danger, and you react in whatever way will make that danger disappear, even if it means going along with things you never wanted to do.

The obligation is not necessarily as negative as fear: We feel obligated to people we love and feel loyalty toward. When we love or are loyal to someone, we feel a certain sense of duty to make sure they are happy, safe, and protected. The narcissist preys upon these feelings of obligation and showers you with gifts and affection to win your affection. Once he has won that spot in your inner circle of friends and family, he knows he can start to tap into your feelings of obligation and use it as a way to manipulate you into doing things in the name of love. After all, if you loved him, you would be willing to do it because you know how much it means to him. In non-romantic relationships, this could involve a relative asking for money or help with childcare with a reminder that family always takes care of its own, or a friend reminding you of that time she bought you something to get you to pay for an expensive meal.

The guilt is employed when the narcissist can see that you are resisting giving in to the sense of obligation. At this stage, the narcissist will blame you for any negative consequences. If he cheated on you because you were unwilling to spend time with him, it is your fault for driving him to that loneliness and had you only been willing to give him whatever he had been asking for, he would not have felt the need to go feel validated with someone else. The person who needed help with childcare may blame you if he loses his job due to not having someone to watch the children.

FOG is frequently employed when the narcissist is grasping at straws. This is a bit more of a long-term manipulation tactic that requires plenty of effort to maintain, as the narcissist must always have something that can be held over your head. This could be the narcissist threatening to take custody of children, or a family member withholding inheritance money.

DARVO (Deny, Attack and Reverse Victim and Offender)

Yet another acronym, DARVO stands for denies, attack, and reverses victim and offender. This is a common reaction when narcissists feel called out. This technique has three steps that follow in a specific order. First, the narcissist denies the claim against him. Next, he attacks the accuser with a statement intended to put the accuser on the defensive. Lastly, he reverses the victim and offender by painting himself as the victim. This manipulation tactic puts the accuser on defensive and removes attention from him.

For example, imagine confronting your narcissistic friend about never being there for you. You may see the following dialogue:

You: "You are never there for me when I need you."

Friend: That's not true. But remember when I fell and broke my foot? You never came to help me. No matter how hard I try, I am never good enough for you and you never want to help me when you feel like I'm an inconvenience."

You can see how, in this dialogue, the narcissist twisted the situation around to benefit her. She denied, and then attacked you with an accusation of not coming to her help when she needed it, and then made herself the victim.

The Silent Treatment

Perhaps more than anything else, narcissists fear a lack of attention. The ultimate lack of attention, to a narcissist, is the silent treatment, and when you have done something that the narcissist is not happy with, she is quick to dole out the silent treatment to make that unhappiness as obvious as possible. Knowing that the ultimate insult to the narcissist is the silent treatment, that is how she goes about showing her displeasure. She seeks to because you distress by ignoring your very existence, looking past you and refusing to even acknowledge you are there. You may not even know why it is happening, but you are left confused and hurt by the exchange or lack thereof, and when the silent treatment is ended, the narcissist comes back as if nothing ever happened. This is especially hurtful in romantic relationships, as you are suddenly dropped, and you do not even have an explanation for why or an idea of whether it is your partner looking for space or ending the relationship entirely. You are left in a sort of emotional limbo as you wait to see if the narcissist will ever return to you.

CHAPTER 6

Narcissist's Target

Narcissists everywhere have similar taste in targets. Because they almost universally rely on manipulation tactics that follow specific patterns, they also tend to seek out the same kinds of people because those tactics work on those people. Certain traits can make for a particularly attractive target for narcissistic abuse, and if you have all five of the ones that are listed, you may find yourself desired by narcissists around you, seeking you out and wanting to abuse your good nature in order to meet their own narcissistic supply. Recognize that not all of the traits listed here are necessarily negative or bad to have, but when combined, they do leave you vulnerable. Understanding which of these traits you may have will help you better protect from narcissistic traps.

Desirable or Attractive Traits or Possessions

Since narcissists only think about themselves, they are only ever doing things if they want something. It could be money, power, status, or attractive partners, or anything else. Regardless of what the narcissist desires, if she finds someone who has what she wants, she will want to pursue a further relationship with him or her. Attracting a narcissist's attention means you have something that the narcissist values and that are the first criteria to be a narcissist's victim. Even if you do not meet the rest of the criteria on this list, just having something desirable means that the narcissist will be more inclined to try to get close to you just to mirror and emulate you. After all, she might be able to get what you have if she acts just like you.

Caregiver

Some people naturally gravitate toward caring for others. They are frequently very empathetic and loving, and their empathy makes them compassionate towards others and their struggles. Because of that compassion and empathy, these people are more inclined to help others in any way they can, even if that involves plenty of patience and understanding, even if some pain is expected along the way.

That compassion, empathy, and patience that caregiver types exhibit is incredibly attractive to narcissists. Narcissists crave attention and admiration, and someone with a caregiver personality is quite likely to happily provide the kind of attention a narcissist needs in the name of taking care of him or her. Knowing that narcissists actively seek out compassionate individuals who thrive on caring for others because they know that these people will see the narcissist as someone in dire need of caring and compassion. They will regard the narcissist with more grace than could ever be deserved and do everything they can to meet the narcissist's needs.

Grew up with Dysfunction

Dysfunctional upbringings cause people to develop skewed senses for what is and is not normal. People often default to what they grew up with as the norm and often repeat what was seen in childhood. When you grow up in a dysfunctional household, you fail to see the glaring red flags around you in the future. For example, if you grew up seeing people who disrespect each other, you normalize that and when you find yourself being sworn at by a narcissist, it seems normal to you. You do not realize that, in healthy relationships, people do not swear at each other or call each other names when the only relationships that were ever modeled for you involved those behaviors. You do not learn to set up normal, healthy boundaries because the people you grew up around failed to set them.

When you have had that dysfunctional way of life modeled and normalized for you, you are far more likely to accept those abusive tendencies in the future simply because you do not know better. Accepting those behaviors for someone you love is an acceptable compromise when you have never seen any different, and because of that, you are an easy target. Because you lack proper boundaries or a proper idea of what a normal relationship is like when you grow up in a dysfunctional home, you are far more likely to seek out something familiar, even if familiar is unhealthy.

Avoids Confrontation

Narcissists are able to get away with their behaviors because oftentimes, those around them are confrontation avoidant. Since the manipulation tactics a narcissist frequently employs require manipulation, which requires the narcissist to avoid being called out in order to work, narcissists tend to gravitate toward people who are uncomfortable with conflict. These people are far more likely to submit and give the narcissist whatever she may desire in the name of avoiding conflict, which works just fine for the narcissist. She wants to find people who will tolerate her manipulation and abuse, even if that tolerance is hesitant or faked. Since, by nature, no confrontational people avoid arguments, they tend to shy away from calling out manipulation or inconsistencies as they happen, and they are likely to tolerate being mistreated because putting up with the manipulation and abuse is seen as more tolerable than creating a conflict. Unfortunately, though no confrontational individuals attempt to avoid conflict at all costs, their peaceful nature tends to attract the attention of those who would love nothing more than to abuse that peacefulness for their own personal gain.

Lacking Self-Esteem

People with low or virtually nonexistent self-esteem crave love and affection. They want to feel special or as though someone loves them, even though they simultaneously feel as though they are worthless or unworthy for some reason. Their low self-esteem leaves them feeling as though they are unimportant or less deserving of success, happiness, love, and family; though these may be the things they crave more than anything else.

Because people with low self-esteem crave that connection and love more than anything, they will frequently put up with abuse because they think it is the only way they will ever receive it. Even though every person is deserving of love, people with low self-esteem do not believe this. This leaves them vulnerable, as when they do find someone who takes a special interest in them, they are willing to go along with anything. Those with low self-esteem are more susceptible to the love-bombing stage and will likely cling to any scraps of perceived affection, even if they come with abuse and negativity. Due to feeling as though no one else could love them because of their perceived faults, they are willing to put up with the abuse of the one person they believe will. Because of that willingness to put up with the abuse, narcissists seek those with low self-esteem out, knowing they will be able to be manipulated into believing that the controlling behaviors are an attempt at showing love and are proof that the narcissist loves them. Those with low self-esteem may even believe that the harsh criticisms are true and that the narcissist is actually trying to help correct for those flaws to help them grow into the person they ought to be. Unfortunately, that could not be further from the truth, and the narcissist only seeks to keep self-esteem at an all-time low for ease of manipulation.

CHAPTER 7

Codependency and Narcissists

Codependency and narcissism are two sides to the same coin. They both lack healthy senses of self and they both struggle with defining who they are, bringing a whole barrage of issues to the table. Ultimately, codependency and narcissism are two different reactions to similar situations. Whereas the narcissist learns to be overtly selfish, the codependent learns to be overtly selfless. However, they are not always strictly opposites, and in some cases, the two can overlap to some degree; someone can exhibit codependent behaviors in certain situations while behaving narcissistically in other contexts. For example, someone could be very codependent in a marriage or relationship, seeking out to cater to their spouse's every whim, but be quite narcissistic with other people, such as friends or strangers. Though narcissism and codependence are both quite different, their root cause is the same.

What is Codependency?

In many normal relationships, we develop dependent relationships. This means that we prioritize our partners and rely on each other for love and in times we need support. The relationship is mutually beneficial, and neither person worries about expressing their true emotions. In a dependent relationship, both people are able to enjoy time spent away from the relationship while still meeting each other's needs.

However, in a codependent relationship, the codependent feels as though his only worth comes from being needed. He will make huge sacrifices, martyring himself out in order to ensure that the other person's needs are met. He only feels worthy if he is able to be needed. He exists solely for the relationship and feels as though he is worthless outside of that relationship. The relationship is his only identity, and he will cling to it at all costs, and within that relationship, he will ignore his own needs and wants, feeling as though they are unimportant.

Someone with codependent tendencies will struggle to detach from his partner because his entire sense of self is wrapped up in aiding that other person. It may get so bad that it begins to negatively impact the codependent's life. The codependent relationship can become all-consuming, taking over the person's life in all areas. Other relationships can weaken and fail as the codependent focuses solely on the person with which the relationship is held. Career potential may be lost, or the codependent may be fired when the relationship begins to interfere with the quality of work. Everyday responsibilities may be shirked in favor of catering to the enabler, the person with whom the codependent is in a relationship. Overall, the entire relationship is built on the faulty ground and is dysfunctional.

Causes of Codependency

Like NPD, there are many external factors that are believed to cause a codependent personality to develop. You may recognize these as being quite like what was discussed as causes for NPD earlier within the book. This is because both codependency and narcissism are similar personality flaws, stemming from the same root cause of damaged self-esteem.

Poor Parental Relationships

Oftentimes, people who have developed a codependent personality have grown up repeatedly having conflicts with their parents throughout childhood. Their parents may have prioritized themselves, or somehow otherwise denied that the child's needs were important. By repeatedly downplaying the child's needs, the child internalizes that those needs are not important enough to meet. After all, if the child's parents could not be bothered to tend to them, they must not matter. The child learns to prioritize his or her parents instead and feel greedy or as though a selfish decision was made when trying to commit to self-care. Oftentimes, this kind of relationship between parent and child happens because the parent has an addiction problem and would do anything to feed the addiction, or the parent never matured past the selfish stage of development as a child and focuses solely on him or herself. Because of all the time spent focusing on the parent's needs, the child never develops the independence and identity necessary to be successful in life. Feeling incomplete when not needed, these people frequently seek out other enablers that will allow them to continue living in this fashion.

Living with Someone Dependent on Care

When a child grows up around someone else who requires frequent or around-the-clock care beyond the realm of normal, whether due to severe illness, injury, or some sort of mental illness, the child's needs may go unmet in favor of meeting more pressing ones. As the child is pushed aside in favor of the person who needs the care, the idea of the child's needs become less important to become internalized. The child may also engage in some of the care for the dependent person as well, causing his needs to be put on the backburner as he takes care of the person who literally cannot care for herself. While living with a family member that requires extra care does not necessarily cause codependency to develop on its own and many people can make it through the caregiving stage without issue, in certain circumstances and with certain personality types that are predisposed to codependent tendencies, it can become an issue. It becomes an issue if the child is younger during the time there is someone dependent on care and the parent of the child tends to focus entirely on the dependent instead of spending the time the child needs to grow and thrive meeting the child's needs.

Abuse

It is no surprise that abuse, regardless of physical, emotional, or sexual, leaves lasting harm on a child. While some children go on to abuse others, others may fall into a pattern of codependency. A child who is exposed to repeated abuse eventually begins to develop a coping mechanism in which she suppresses her feelings. She begins to ignore and cast aside the pain that is felt because of the abuse, and this ultimately teaches her to ignore her own needs later in life. This leaves her only caring about other people's needs while neglecting her own.

Abuse victims also tend to seek out people with similar tendencies as the abuser as this is what is familiar. They know how to live through the abuse and understand that the relationship will often revolve around the codependent behaviors. Abusers and narcissists love codependents, as codependents will tolerate vast amounts of abuse that would make other people balk.

Key Features of Codependency

Oftentimes, codependency manifests in ways that are incredibly recognizable. Though every person is different and the behaviors will change depending on the relationship, there are several behavioral patterns associated with codependency. Knowing how to identify these will enable you to recognize when you or someone you know is exhibiting codependent tendencies. If you feel as though you yourself may be codependent, seeking the professional opinion from a trained psychologist would be a great place to start on your journey toward understanding yourself.

- **Exaggerated Sense of Responsibility:** Codependents frequently feel as though the weight of their loved one's actions is on their shoulders. They feel as though they are directly responsible for the actions of their partners, children, or anyone else with which they are codependent.

- **Confuse Love and Pity:** Codependents think that pitying and desiring to help someone is the same as love. They think that every time they feel compelled to rescue someone, they are doing it out of love instead of out of compassion for another human being.

- **Doing More Than Their Fair Share:**
Codependents tend to bear the burden of work, even
when the share is more than unfair. They feel as though
they have to take the burden in order to support or
protect their enabler, who typically is more than happy
to allow the codependent to do so, even when it may be
detrimental to the codependent to take that added
burden.

- **Sensitive When Good Deeds are Unrecognized:**
When a codependent feels as though her efforts have
gone ignored, she is likely to feel hurt or as though she
was not good enough. She will try to further martyr
herself to get the recognition she craves to soothe her
low self-esteem and prove that she matters.

- **Feeling Guilty When Caring for Self:** Any time the
codependent engages in acts she may see as selfish or
unnecessary in the grand scheme of things, she will feel
guilty. After all, her needs ought to be met last, and if
she does anything other than that, she is behaving
selfishly, and that is absolutely unacceptable to her.

- **Rigid:** Codependents do not tolerate change. They
often seek out things that are familiar for this reason,
which leads them to constantly seek out other enablers

in relationships, even if those enablers prove to be abusive.

- **Cannot Set Healthy Boundaries:** Codependents see no boundaries between themselves and their enablers. They have no sense of self that is outside of the relationship or apart from the enabler. Because they fail to set boundaries, the relationship eventually consumes their lives and leaves little room for anything else. This lack of boundaries also leads to needs going unmet.

- **Needs Recognition to Feel Whole:** Without recognition for good deeds and caring for others, codependents feel unwanted and unimportant. They require people to recognize their actions in order to help bolster their fragile self-esteem.

- **Need to Control Others:** Codependents, feeling utterly responsible for the actions of their enablers, also seek some level of control over the relationships. Because the codependents always do everything possible for the enablers, they develop that control they desire, and the enabler allows them to have it. Without control, the codependents feel unable to help.

- **Fear of Abandonment:** With their sub-par self-esteem and feeling as though they have no sense of identity beyond their relationship, codependents are terrified of being abandoned. They will do anything in their power to keep the relationship going.

- **Poor Decision-making Skills:** Oftentimes, their dysfunctional opinion and view of their relationships make the codependents make bad decisions. These could range from refusing to leave a dangerous situation because they want to stay with their partner, or refusing to meet their needs, even if it makes them sick or gets them hurt.

- **Difficulty Communicating:** Codependents struggle to communicate their own needs and wants because they are so caught up in the idea that they do not matter. Even if they hate something, they will refuse to say it if they think it would be detrimental, even slightly, to the other person.

- **Unhealthy Dependence on Relationship:** Codependents exist solely for their relationships and enablers, and that dependence on their enablers crosses the line into the territory of dysfunction.

- **Untrusting:** Oftentimes due to so much dysfunction in childhood, codependents tend to distrust those around them, especially those who insist that their needs should be met or that try to point out that their relationship is unhealthy.

- **Confrontation-Avoidant:** Codependents avoid confrontation at all costs. They have developed their tendency to avoid their own needs due to wanting to avoid confrontation, and that tendency to avoid confrontation has extended well into adulthood. The codependent will do anything to avoid a conflict, especially with the enabler.

Codependents and Narcissists

As you have read about codependents and their tendencies, it should become obvious that codependents make the ultimate target for the narcissist. They meet each and every line on the narcissist's guide to choosing a target, and they are the ultimate victim for the narcissist. In a partnership between a codependent and a narcissist, the codependent gives endlessly to the narcissist, who needs the attention to feel loved, and the narcissist gets to give the codependent the gift of being needed. Both the narcissist and the codependent get their dysfunctional needs met. While this may seem like the perfect arrangement, it still encourages two people to live incredibly unhealthy lives. The codependent never has basic needs met and still has broken self-esteem and lacks an identity. The narcissist never gives back in the relationship and continues to live in the delusion that the narcissist is the only one that matters. The narcissist's own self-esteem and disordered thinking are not fixed through being catered to. This leads to an interesting relationship in which both the narcissist and the codependent enable each other.

Furthermore, this relationship leads to the codependent wanting to live through the narcissist. When the narcissist is not appreciative of the codependent's behaviors, which he will never be because he does not recognize other people's needs, the codependent may feel slighted or unappreciated. Over time, these patterns may lead to resentment, but the codependent will continue trekking through the relationship, martyring her to him because that is what she feels is the right thing to do. The narcissist typically will begin to exploit the codependent more and more over time, seeking out more narcissistic supply without ever returning the sentiment with any appreciation that the codependent needs. The codependent eventually reaches a point of giving up, but despite this, neither partner is likely to leave. The narcissist loves the easy access to narcissistic supply and having someone willing to cater to his every whim, and the codependent wants to feel needed, even though there is no appreciation reciprocated. Even if the relationship teeters toward abusive, neither partner is likely to leave, nor does the relationship become even more toxic and dysfunctional.

CHAPTER 8

Dealing with a Narcissist

Dealing with a narcissist is incredibly difficult in the best of times, but there are many different ways to manage your relationship. Regardless of whether you are interested in severing all ties for good or you are in a position of having to continue some degree of contact with a narcissist, understanding some of the ways to deal with the narcissist's toxic behaviors can help you minimize your risks of harm and abuse. You can also cause the narcissist to lose interest in you and move on to other targets when you prove yourself invulnerable to his manipulative tactics.

Keep in mind that this will be a trial and error effort, and not every method discussed here may be useful or productive in your unique situation. Consider each method carefully to decide if it meets your needs and can help you, and once you have chosen a method, it is important to remember to keep it up. No matter how much the narcissist may push and try to get your attention back, be consistent in order to get the best effect from your actions. None of these methods are easy, and each will take a gargantuan amount of effort, but when you finally make it to the other side and realize how very free you are from the narcissist's abuse, you will recognize that it was worth every ounce of effort you put into it.

Cutting off the Narcissist

The easiest way to avoid harm from a narcissist is to end the relationship entirely. Refuse to engage in the relationship at all costs. Taking a huge step back from the relationship may be necessary so you can clear your head and see things for what they are. This is typically a permanent change and decision and is the only surefire way to make sure that the narcissistic abuse stops. If you refuse to play the game at all, the narcissist cannot manipulate you.

Furthermore, by refusing any sort of engagement or communication with the narcissist, you are able to deny the narcissist's strongest motivator: Your attention. You suddenly remove yourself as a reliable source of narcissistic supply, and if you continue to deny the narcissist, ultimately, he will have to go elsewhere to meet his need.

Keep in mind that when you do this method, there will be a period that, in psychology, is called an extinction burst. Consider an experiment in which a rat is taught to press a button to get a small nibble of candy. The rat very quickly learns to expect that candy every time the button is pressed, and the behavior of pressing a button becomes positively reinforced. The rat does this to get the candy and does so repeatedly. If the rate goes up and presses the button and one day, it just stops giving out candy, the rat will be confused. It will press the button again and again, with increasing fervor, as it desperately tries to force the button to do what was expected of it and provide more candy. Over time, the rat will lose interest when it becomes clear there is no further reaction, but it will go back to the button occasionally and try to press the button.

Think of the narcissist as the rat and the narcissistic supply as the candy. You are the button to get it. As soon as you cut off contact, the narcissist will suddenly resort to every last strategy that has proven successful in the past in order to try to get your attention and that narcissistic supply desired. He will attempt everything, ranging from love bombs to promises of change and even threats of abuse or suicide if you do not give in. The most important thing to remember is that you cannot give in. No matter what the narcissist says or does, refuse to give him what he wants. His behaviors will escalate more, just like a toddler throwing a fit over having routine broken unexpectedly, and he will not stop at anything that he thinks will be effective. Eventually, however, you will weather the storm, and the narcissist will stop trying. The need for narcissistic supply is too strong, and he will seek it out elsewhere if you continue to refuse. At that point, remember that he will likely come back again in the future to try again, but each attempt will be weaker than the last as he learns that it is useless.

Remember, the period of leaving an abusive relationship is the most dangerous, and the narcissist likely will rely on every physical and emotional threat he can think of. He may threaten to kill himself, you, or other people, or he may begin stalking you. No matter what he does, refuse to engage, and report erratic or dangerous behavior to the appropriate authorities.

Take a Break from the Relationship

Similar to cutting off the narcissist, taking a break from the relationship involves a refusal to communicate. In this case, however, it is not permanent. The break is intended to allow you to clear your head and reevaluate whether you want to continue the relationship. Regardless of what he may accuse you of, remind yourself that this is not a punishment. You did not make this decision to hurt him; you made it protect and care for yourself. You are entitled to controlling who you communicate with, and if you decide that you do not want to talk to the narcissist, you are within your rights to make that choice.

When taking a break from the narcissist, it is appropriate to tell him once that you are taking a break and you will discuss things with him when you are ready. You do not have to provide him with a timeline, no matter how much he may pester you for one, and at that point, you refuse all future contact. You are giving yourself the chance to cool off. You are ensuring that you do not say something that will make the situation worse or inflame the narcissist into doing something harmful.

Do not let the narcissist goad you into responses with accusations of abuse or through playing the victim. You are making a choice that works for you, and ultimately that is the most important part. You need the breathing room and you are taking it. Remind yourself that you owe it to yourself to care for yourself, especially when no one else will. You cannot care for others if you are not caring for yourself.

Healthy Boundaries

Sometimes, cutting off a narcissist is not a viable option, and that is okay. When you have no choice but to continue contact, such as if you are bound by court order to continue a co-parenting relationship, or you work with the narcissist and are not in a position to leave your job, you can focus on mitigating as much harm as possible and protecting yourself from the toxicity the narcissist seems to naturally exude.

Healthy boundaries are one of the easiest techniques to minimize harm from a narcissist, but they are difficult. These boundaries represent a line between what is acceptable and unacceptable to you, and they are to be set at your own prerogative. Boundaries are a healthy part of every relationship, regardless of whether it is a marriage, a friendship, or even with your children. Without boundaries, you will find yourself constantly stepping on toes and breeding resentment.

Unfortunately, narcissists see boundaries as the ultimate insult. It is irresistible to the narcissist, and he will try to stomp on them at every turn. The boundaries set are nothing more than challenges; games to get rises out of you and exert control over your emotional state. When you set these boundaries, you must be prepared to enforce and defend them at all costs.

When the narcissist challenges a boundary, give him one warning. Tell him that if he continues to test your boundary, you will provide a consequence. Tell the narcissist what that consequence for stomping on your boundary is, and every time it is done, you need to enforce the consequence. If you tell the narcissist that you will take an extended break in the event that your boundary is broken, follow through when he stomps on it. If you tell him you will stop talking to the narcissist if he calls you names in anger and he calls you names, you must immediately disengage and walk away. The key here is to follow through with the entire consequence, no matter how much the narcissist may cry, beg, or threaten.

Disengage

When cutting off is not an option, the next best thing is disengaging emotionally. If you do not invest any emotional energy into your interactions with the narcissist, he will eventually lose interest in you. You can keep your interactions relatively unchanged, but do not pay any attention to the words said, no matter how hurtful they may be. Try to keep in mind that people with NPD are stuck in a developmental stage of a child, unable to feel empathy and wired to be selfish, and remind yourself that if a child had said the things the narcissist spewed at you, you would likely not be very upset or offended at all. After all, children are impulsive, emotional, and irrational. The narcissist hits all three of those traits on the nose, and you should not take the narcissist's actions personally at all.

Disengaging does not mean ignoring or bottling your feelings, however. When you disengage, acknowledge what was said and give it the consideration it deserves, which is, admittedly, very little. This can be particularly difficult if the narcissist is a loved one that you trusted but remember to try to disregard the emotional reactions to the words protects you. You do not fall into the narcissist's trap, and you do not let the narcissist regain control over your emotions, and in return, the narcissist will slowly lose interest.

The Grey Rock Method

Similar to disengaging emotionally, the grey rock method involves minimizing emotional reactions, but in this case, it is ignoring all interactions, both good and bad. You are aiming to avoid as much interaction as possible, and when you are forced to interact, you should keep it boring and meaningless. The name alludes to a grey rock on the side of the road. Consider how often you notice and remember all of the rocks you walk past in a given day—the answer is most likely none. People do not pay attention to something as mundane and worthless as a grey rock on the side of the road. Your goal in this method is to be as mundane and useless to the narcissist as the grey rock. If you can achieve this state of mediocrity, the narcissist will slowly lose interest in you.

The trick in interacting is to tell you to be robotic in responses. No matter how angry you may feel in response to whatever was said, respond in as few words as possible, and make sure it is never immediately after the message was sent if it does not warrant an immediate response. For example, imagine that he messaged you saying that you are beautiful and he loves you. This should be ignored. Five minutes later, he messages asking how your shared child is doing. Give him the bare minimum answer while still being comprehensive. List what she is doing, whether she is sick, and maybe what she ate for dinner, but keep the interaction as emotionless as possible.

Do not emote, no matter how tempting it may be.

Be Realistic

Keeping your interactions with the narcissist realistic will keep you from setting up high standards that she will never meet. Telling yourself that she will never be emotionally supportive with you and that it is a personality limit that she lacks empathy will help you keep reality in mind when dealing with a narcissist. If you are fully prepared for the narcissist to respond in typical narcissist fashion, you will always be prepared, no matter how she responds, and you may even find that you are surprised on occasion. This is key when you are maintaining a relationship with a narcissist, whether romantic, platonic, workplace, familial, or co-parenting. You are protected from the disappointment of narcissistic behavior.

Keep in mind that being realistic does not excuse abuse. It is never okay for someone to hurt you or step on your boundaries. However, if you know that narcissists do those, you will not be as blindsided when it does happen, and you can better prepare in advance to protect yourself. You should absolutely still correct negative or unproductive behaviors, even if it is unpleasant or you would rather avoid doing so.

Focus on the Positive

Likewise, when continuing to interact with a narcissist,

remembering to focus on the positive can aid you in recognizing things that you enjoy about the person. After all, something must have attracted you to the narcissist at some point, and you may be happy to see tiny semblances of that person in the narcissist in front of you. While the personality is still likely vastly different from the one you met at first, there still may be parts of the narcissist that at least make her tolerable. For example, she may be horrible at being emotional support or anything but the center of attention, but she may also genuinely be a good cook, and she loves to cook for all of your friends' get-togethers, or she may be incredibly smart and you enjoy the intellectual conversations you have over coffee, even if they involve occasional snide comments about how you do not understand because you did not go to school for politics, or whatever the two of you were discussing. Reminding yourself of the positives can help you in moments when you are ready to lose your temper with the narcissist, but it would be detrimental to do so.

Decide Your Hill Die On

The last important tactic to remember is to choose your hill to die on wisely. This is a fancy way of saying choose your battles carefully. Though narcissists seek out confrontation-avoidant people on purpose, choosing to avoid conflict can actually be a way to avoid detection too. For this reason, you should always pick your battles wisely and only be prepared to engage in a conflict if you truly want to deal with the aftermath. While some things are absolutely worthy of a conflict, such as a co-parent choosing to drive with children in the car while drunk, an argument over who said something first is petty, and the narcissist are not likely to ever concede or admit that he is lying. For this reason, you should only choose battles if you are willing to fight for them. If you are unwilling to deal with the aftermath and ultimately, whatever the narcissist did is insignificant, do not bother fighting over it.

CHAPTER 9

Narcissistic Abuse

Narcissistic abuse is insidious, slowly penetrating every part of your life. The longer you feel trapped in the abuse, the more lost you become, until eventually; you are just floating through life, a mere shell of the beautiful, personable individual you were before entangling yourself with a narcissist. Little by little, the narcissist broke you down, until one day, you no longer recognize yourself in the mirror. While narcissistic abuse is incredibly damaging, it does not have to be permanent, and you can recover from its effects, though you may always bear some of the scars left by the wounds. If you feel as though you might be in a narcissistic relationship loaded with abuse, this chapter will provide you with the telltale signs and put names to the various types of abuse you may have faced. Please remember, no abuse is worth tolerating, and no matter what anyone else has said, no one deserves to be abused. You deserve happiness and healthiness, and you can attain it. If you feel as though you are being abused and you need help immediately, do not hesitate to reach out to other people around you, or to call your emergency services or your local domestic abuse hotline. There is help available to you and you do not have to be trapped any longer than you already have been.

Types of Abuse

Narcissistic abuse comes in many different forms, and some of them may surprise you. Many behaviors that you may have seen as controlling or that made you uncomfortable may actually be types of abuse that you have overlooked for too long due to a lack of physical evidence of your abuse. Keep in mind that not every type of abuse has to be physical, and there are many other kinds that can leave far worse scars than a fist can. If you are experiencing any of these, understand that you are well within your rights to leave, and leaving is the healthier option. You are not forced to live in an abusive situation, no matter how afraid of failing to live on your own you may be.

Verbal Abuse

Verbal abuse entails yelling, belittling, or any other type of verbal put-downs. These are said with the intention of tearing you down as opposed to be some sort of negative, but still constructive, criticism, and verbal abuse should not be overlooked just because it does not leave physical marks. This may involve name-calling, insults, telling you how useless you are, criticizing you, attacking you, interrupting you, and any other intentionally harmful use of a voice. Even demands, threats, and sarcasm are forms of verbal abuse. In order to decide if something is a form of verbal abuse, consider the context and whether it was malicious. If contextually, it was said to hurt you, then it is likely verbal abuse. If it was something that put you down but was meant to be of benefit to you, it may not have been.

Manipulation

As discussed in depth, manipulation is one of the narcissist's favorite games. They love to exert control over you, pulling your strings to get their desired results with just the right amount of deniability. Oftentimes, these manipulative tactics are done in a way where it seems harmless to outsiders, but you feel it in your gut that it was hostile or demeaning. Trust your gut reaction.

Emotional Abuse

Emotional abuse involves punishments, threats, intimidation, silent treatment, or other acts that sway your emotions. It is meant to belittle you and keep you in fear. This is intended to trigger the FOG response, keeping you stuck in the loop of fear, obligation, and guilt. It also involves playing with your emotions, such as building you up with love bombing only to suddenly tear that love and affection away in the blink of an eye. Anything that toys with your emotions are a form of emotional abuse.

Physical Abuse

This is perhaps the most obvious of the abuse tactics used by narcissists. Any abuse that physically harms you or keeps you trapped in a form of physical abuse. There may be displays of aggression, such as punching doors or walls, or acts of holding you in place when you want to leave. If the other party's hands are ever on you without your consent, it is physical abuse.

Sexual Abuse

Even in romantic relationships and marriages, sexual abuse is an issue to contend with. Just because you are married or have consented to sexual acts in the past does not mean that your permission is indefinite. Some narcissists will use this to keep control over you or to serve their own needs when you are reluctant.

Neglect

Neglect is typically considered in the context of a child with a narcissistic parent, though it could be seen in other contexts too if the narcissist is in a position of providing everything needed to survive but has refused to do so. In the context of children, this can include leaving the child in a dangerous situation or starving.

Financial Abuse

Financial abuse entails withholding all money or the vast majority of the money, and only providing the victim with a small amount, or in some cases, none at all, even if the victim is the one who earned it. This is to keep the victim dependent on the narcissist for everything, enabling easier manipulation in the future. This can be done through threats, theft, or even using your name and private information to take out credit cards in your name and build up debt with them.

Isolation

Isolation involves putting a gap between the victim and anyone that may be a support system for the victim. Your contact with the outside world may be restricted in order to grant the narcissist a more complete control, but also to ensure that the abuse is not discovered.

Signs of Abuse

People who are abused by narcissists often report similar signs and symptoms of the abuse. While not every person will follow this pattern exactly, many people will exhibit some of these symptoms if they have been exposed to systematic and regular narcissistic abuse.

Feeling Detached

Detaching yourself is a form of a defense mechanism called dissociation. In this state, you feel detached from your emotions, and in some cases, your body. It is one of the more defining features of experiencing trauma and is frequently seen in survivors of narcissistic abuse. The mind tries to sequester the traumatic event away to try to cope with it, but this can have some serious implications, as you may begin to fragment yourself into multiple pieces just to cope with the abuse you have endured, and you may begin to experience altered levels of consciousness and see effects to your memory.

Walking on Eggshells

Those who have lived through trauma often go out of their ways to avoid anything even remotely associated with the trauma. You may constantly start avoiding people that remind you of your abuser or being careful to avoid saying some of the phrases he used frequently to avoid feeling a sense of being triggered. You may begin watching what you do or say around your abuser in hopes of avoiding another bout of abuse, but you likely still are his target. This leaves you feeling anxious most of the time, with that sensation of walking on eggshells as you desperately try to avoid setting your abuser off.

Self-Sacrificing

Through being abused and having none of your needs met for an extended period of time, you have given up on meeting your own wants and needs. Your goals and desires are cast aside in favor of catering to the narcissist, ensuring that you never upset or trigger him in an attempt to avoid further abuse. Ultimately, you are left without ambitions or hobbies, having let your entire self be consumed by the narcissist for his own personal gain.

Health Issues Related to Psychological Distress

Oftentimes, your psychological distress manifests physically. Your weight may have fluctuated drastically, or your body, overwhelmed by stress, has begun to show signs of aging or you find yourself getting sicker than you ever have before. Abuse raises cortisol levels as you stress, which suppresses your immune system. Your sleep is interrupted by trauma, which further raises your stress levels.

Distrustful

After being betrayed so thoroughly by someone you once trusted or loved, you find yourself constantly feeling threatened from all sides. You trust nobody around you and seek to protect yourself by remaining hypervigilant around all others, even when the people around you may have given you no signs that they would harm you.

Self-Harm or Thoughts of Suicide

As depression and anxiety develop in the face of abuse, you may find yourself having thoughts of harming yourself or of committing suicide. You feel as though suicide may be the only real way out of your situation and find yourself struggling to cope. You get to the point that you feel like death is favorable to living any longer trapped with your abuser. Remember, if you are having these suicidal thoughts, or thoughts of harming yourself, you are having a medical emergency. Please seek help as soon as possible to help yourself stabilize so you can get yourself out of the situation that drove you this far in the first place.

Self-Isolating

While the abuser frequently engages in isolating the victim in order to keep the abuse hidden, the abuse victim also may engage in self-isolation. After feeling shame for suffering through abuse or feeling as though you have let yourself get into this situation, you may be afraid or embarrassed to let other people know about your situation in fear of having them judge you. Especially in a social climate that seems to favor abusers and blame the victim, you may be afraid of stepping out and asking for help, so you instead turn inward and refuse to see anyone.

Blaming Yourself

It is easy to blame yourself for being stupid enough to get trapped in such a bad relationship in the first place when you find yourself suffering through narcissistic abuse. However, keep in mind that you did not ask to be abused, and you did not deserve it. The narcissist is skilled at manipulating people into seeing what he wants them to see and you fell for it, as did others, and as others will do in the future. This is not a flaw with you; it reflects solely on the narcissist.

Self-Sabotage

Victims of abuse frequently find themselves developing an inner voice that reflects that of their abuser. The victim develops shame related to the situation, and in many cases, self-sabotages due to a perceived sense of worthlessness. Because the abuser has beaten the victim down so much, the victim has come to accept the narcissist's narrative of the world surrounding them.

Living in Fear

Narcissists take offense any time anyone around them is experiencing joy or success, and oftentimes, it is during those periods of success or happiness in which the narcissist escalates, punishing anyone who dares to have something to be happy about. This causes the victim of the narcissistic abuse to develop a fear of success or enjoyment. The fearful disposition also allows for the narcissist to continue to remain the center of attention with less competition.

Protecting the Abuser

Oftentimes, the victim feels some twisted need to protect the abuser from the consequences of such heinous actions. This is a coping mechanism that is meant to help assuage the cognitive dissonance that only someone who has been abused by a person declaring love can understand. The victim may feel as though there is a need to protect the narcissist due to obligation and because the narcissist claims to love the victim. The victim usually takes a share of the blame and says that things are not as bad as they seem due to feeling as though the victim will be unable to survive without the narcissist there to help.

Results of Abuse

Ultimately, even after initially escaping abuse, you may notice the long-lasting effects of living with such a toxic monster. Remember, this is not a reflection of you, but of the abuse, you endured, and it will take time and effort for you to work past these hurdles and become the person you deserve to be. The most frequently noticed behavioral habits after having escaped a narcissist's abuse are echoism and some mental health disorders.

Echoism

In the Greek myth of Narcissus and Echo, Echo was cursed. She was only able to repeat what was said to her last, and as she fell in love with Narcissus, she was only able to repeat what he had said. He did not love her back, and ultimately, cursed to repeat his words; she faded away and died, leaving behind only her voice, which would echo anyone who called out around her.

Like the nymph, Echo, those suffering from echoism fail to develop a sense of self or have that sense of self eroded away. Typically, the most empathetic and emotionally sensitive people, those who become echoes feel as though they have left behind their identities. They put their needs last, ultimately developing a fear of having needs in the first place. They feel as though having needs and acting upon them is enough to prove that they are selfish, though that is just a projection tactic the narcissist has used to convince the victim to forsake her own needs for his sake. Echoism is the ultimate sense of people pleasing, and these people suffer, even after leaving the relationship altogether, as the internalized belief that the victim cannot seek to engage in self-care or have any sort of identity away from the narcissist is ingrained.

Mental Health Issues

Those who have suffered from NPD, especially when it was particularly toxic, may find themselves suffering from other mental health issues. The constant strain of trying to satisfy the insatiable narcissist can develop into anxiety and depression, both of which take their tolls on the individual. Constantly having needs gone unmet and receiving criticism if you dare attempt to voice discontent or that you need something can lead to both anxieties at confrontation or a feeling of depression as you come to believe that the situation is hopeless. Through repeated trauma, you may even develop post-traumatic stress disorder, particularly when the abuse suffered from the narcissist is particularly bad.

Ultimately, leaving a narcissistic abuser is the only true way to avoid harm and protect yourself and your mental health. The longer you are in the relationship, the harder it gets to let go as the trauma-bonding makes leaving seem like an impossibility. Despite the abuse, you feel as though life could not happen any other way, and you find yourself stuck. Remember that you do not have to remain in such a relationship and leaving is always an option.

CHAPTER 10

Healing from Narcissistic Abuse

Narcissistic abuse leaves behind undeniable marks on a person's psyche. It can break you down, turning you into someone you barely even recognize in the mirror, and that realization can be heartbreaking. Do not forget that healing from narcissistic abuse is absolutely possible. With time, effort, and perseverance, you will be able to recover yourself.

No matter how long you were in that relationship or how much abuse you have endured, there is always hope for healing. It will never be easy, but the results will be undeniable. You will feel better as you heal yourself, and soon, those feelings of hopelessness and worthlessness will fade. Step by step, you will be able to get through your healing. Remember that the effort will be worthwhile, and though it will be difficult, you will be able to become someone you are proud of. You deserve the peace of mind and a life of happiness, no matter how much anyone has told you otherwise.

Acknowledgment and Forgiveness

The first step to healing is acknowledging what has happened. You need to recognize that the narcissist hurt you, and you need to be able to see it as the abuse it was. Through labeling it, you erase any pretense that you deserved it or caused it to happen. People do not ask to be abused by a loved one, and your actions or inactions would not have changed the narcissist's penchant for abuse. You need to be able to separate yourself from the abuse and remove the blame from your shoulders in order to begin healing from it.

Remember, you are only responsible for your own actions. You do not control the narcissist, nor did you cause the narcissist to hurt you. Nothing you did made you deserve of the abuse, and if anything, some of your best traits were used to take advantage of you. You were targeted because of your traits as empathetic, attentive, and peaceful. Your best traits made you an unfortunate target, and you should not be ashamed of that.

Acknowledgment of the situation lends itself to forgiving yourself. You will be able to apologize to yourself for not getting out of the situation when the first red flags presented, and to treat yourself with kindness. Your trust was taken advantage of, and in turn, you may have developed self-destructive tendencies in which you blamed yourself for all of it. Letting go of that blame you have developed is crucial to healing.

This forgiveness may be difficult at first but remind yourself that there is no use in dwelling in the past. You cannot change it, no matter how much you may want to, but you can change the course of your future. You can give yourself the life you deserve and break that cycle of abuse by working on yourself. You deserve that forgiveness, and you will feel better as you break away from the blame and guilt the narcissist used to keep you down.

Giving Yourself Time to Grieve

Sometimes, victims of abuse find themselves missing their abusers. They then feel guilty for missing the relationship they thought they had and use it as justification that the abuse endured was deserved or was not as bad as they thought because if it were bad, they feel like they would not have developed the feelings of love, to begin with. Remember, it is okay to be sad about the relationship, and it is absolutely acceptable to grieve it if that is what you need to recover. You did not get the partner or parent or another family member that you deserved, and it is okay to grieve the loss of that ideal person in that role.

When you grieve, you go through five stages. You start in denial, in which you feel as though the relationship does not have to end. You convince yourself that the problems are not as bad as they are in an attempt to save yourself from the heartbreak. Next, you reach anger, in which you finally confront the truth. You recognize the narcissist that has abused you for the monster he or she is, and you feel enraged. You see the abuse clearly and it is enough to stir up some of your most vulnerable feelings. The very thought of your abuser is enough to make you feel that rage. You hate that this has happened, and you feel nothing but raw fury toward the situation. The third step is bargaining, in which you try to come up with reasons or ways you could remain in the relationship. You tell yourself that if you tried a little harder, or worked a little more, or gave up a little bit more of yourself, the abuse would stop and the relationship could continue. Your narcissistic spouse would not berate you if you kept the home cleaner, or if you lost some weight. Your narcissistic mother would love you if you let her spend more time with your children. Continuing to martyr yourself begins to feel like a viable option to return to some semblance of normalcy. The next step is depression. You see that the relationship can never recover, as the person that you loved is incapable of changing. You realize the lack of hope and that things are irrevocably damaged, and this brings about a period of depression. Lastly, as the fog from depression clears, you finally arrive at acceptance. You accept the reality of your situation, and while you may still feel sad about it, you are able to live with it.

Discovering an Outlet for Feelings

As an empath, you may have absorbed some of the narcissist's emotions that can create problems for you. Narcissists love empaths because they are willing to help assuage those negative feelings they sense in the narcissist, but the downside is that those feelings get internalized. To a sensitive empath, those feelings can fester, and even after separating yourself from the narcissist, you may still feel the toxicity swirling within you. For this reason, finding some sort of outlet for your negative feelings is absolutely essential to healing from narcissistic abuse. As the negativity is released, you are able to regain the clarity you had prior to being abused. When choosing an outlet, the most important thing is to make it something that helps you. This could be anything— something creative like painting or writing, or dance, or working out. The important part is releasing all of the negativity welling up within you in a way that works for you. Anything goes, so long as it is beneficial to you.

Creating a Support Network

People thrive when they have others to support them in their toughest times. Finding others who understand you and your struggle can make a huge difference in your time recovering from narcissistic abuse. While you may feel alone, you are far from it, and there are others, just like you, trying to recover from their own narcissistic abusers, and if you can find them, you will find yourself surrounded with people who really understand your situation. These people know what you are going through because they have been there, and that special kind of insight will prove invaluable in your journey.

Not only will you be able to speak with others who understand you, but you will also be able to see people further along in their journey than you are. You will see people who have healed or may be enjoying the lives they have built away from narcissists. These people will provide you with hope and motivation that things will get better, no matter how hard it may be in the moment. With these people as your reminder of the good to come and the support that is there to hold you up in your moments of weakness, you will be able to get through your healing process.

While it may seem daunting to find other people who understand you, do not forget that you have the entirety of the internet at your disposal. You can locate in-person support groups in your area, and even if there are none available to you, you will be able to find plenty of social media or online forum groups dedicated to victims and survivors of narcissistic abuse. While this will not provide face-to-face interaction, you can still forge bonds with those who understand you. This also ups your chances of finding someone whose situation more closely resembles yours. You can likely find someone who has gone through similar abuse, which can provide you with extra insight into your situation. Just because there may be less or no physical contact between you and the person you will meet in an online support group does not mean that your support would be any less meaningful.

Self-Reflection

Essential to ensure that you never fall victim to another narcissist in the future, self-reflection involves understanding how you may have contributed to the situation. This does not mean you would take on the blame or that you were deserving, but it does mean you can recognize how you may have been able to do something to be less vulnerable or less tolerant. This enables you to work toward becoming healthier individual overall.

Perhaps you discover that you were so tolerant because you tried to give your partner the benefit of the doubt and expected that the abusive tendencies were the result of outside stress. Maybe you recognize that you were so desperate to find someone that loves you that you were willing to tolerate anything so long as you were together. Regardless of what the reason for accepting the abuse for so long was, understanding and learning from it will allow you to avoid making the same mistake in the future.

When you are ready to engage in the self-reflection to identify why you were susceptible in the first place, you should make sure you have a quiet area free of distractions and an ample amount of time to really delve into your thoughts and feelings. This is made easier through a journal of sorts to track your thought processes and for future reference. When you have prepared, take a deep, cleansing breath, and begin to think about what is causing you pain at that moment. It is likely related to the narcissist in some way. Perhaps it was the abuse the narcissist inflicted. Write that down and begin pondering why that made you feel the way it did. Describe exactly what the abuse made you feel and why it mattered to you. Write down anything that comes to mind as you do this, and though it may be difficult and you may find yourself crying or hurting, you should continue going for as long as you can manage. Write down every feeling, observation, opinion, and thought that come to mind, and let each be validated. No matter how silly you may think they are, write them down. Later, you can reread these thoughts to see where your mind is. You will be able to identify sensitive topics and weaknesses with the intention of correcting them in the future.

Self-Care

After so long catering to the narcissist, you are long overdue for some self-care of your own. This is a crucial step in your healing, as you are finally reclaiming yourself and your priorities. Make it a point to engage in self-care daily. This can be anything: Exercising more or spending time creating art.

Anything that makes you feel better about yourself, physically or emotionally. After so long being crippled by the narcissist, you finally have the opportunity to flourish and grow into the person you can be.

Therapy

When you are left to cope with deep-rooted trauma after suffering at the hands of a narcissist for so long, therapy can be a fantastic way to unpack it all. Guided by a licensed professional, you will be able to cope better with your feelings and may even learn some new ways to cope at the moment when things get tough. This can help you learn the ways you may have been sensitive or vulnerable but also provide you with the help and guidance you need to correct for it. If therapy seems like something you would benefit from, speak to your doctor to get a referral to a local therapist that may be beneficial to you.

Compassion

The most important facet of your healing, however, will be your compassion toward yourself. While you may be well-versed in treating others with compassion, treating yourself the same may be difficult for you, especially after the narcissist's abuse. Remember to reward yourself with patience and kindness as you recognize that you are healing from some massive trauma. You should also remember that making mistakes is normal and human. While you may have learned to avoid making them due to your time with the narcissist, it is okay for you to make them. Even if you find yourself taking a few steps backward in your progress, you can still get yourself back on track. Have the compassion to recognize that you are not failing just because of a slip-up and that you do not deserve to treat yourself harshly just because you are struggling or finding yourself missing the narcissist. Treat yourself with the kindness and compassion you would show a stranger as you get through his stage of your life. If you fall, you can pick yourself back up and continue on. At the end of the day, you are one step further on your journey, no matter what the situation looks like around you.

CONCLUSION

Congratulations! You have made it to the end of this book. You have learned about what to expect from a narcissist, how to identify whether you are being abused, and how to avoid the narcissist's manipulation. This was the biggest step of your journey toward healing. From here, you are ready to begin implementing the lessons taught in this book. You can begin taking steps toward cutting off or dealing with the narcissist in question and recognizing the abuse and manipulation as it occurs. As you begin disentangling yourself from the narcissist to protect yourself, remember that this may be one of the most difficult things you will ever do, especially if you love him or her.

Do not forget that the past and present situation does not have to be indicative of the future: You can choose to change your path toward something better, toward something you deserve. You deserve to be treated with love, respect, compassion, and consideration of your needs. You deserve nothing but happiness and safety. You deserve to enjoy your life and the people you keep close to you, and you deserve to have a healthy relationship with your loved ones.

Be gentle as you get through this period of time. You are not weak for ending the relationship, nor are you weak if you seek help or ask for support. You deserve that support if you need it and it does not reflect badly upon yourself. Ultimately, the only person who looks bad in this situation is the narcissist. The narcissist, despite the façade, is a broken individual, incapable of loving others or having meaningful relationships. This is not a flaw with you, but rather a flaw with the narcissist. Nothing you have done warranted the abuse he showered you with, nor did you cause him or her to be abusive.

As you continue this journey, keep this book and the advice within it close. Remember that it is okay to be afraid of the future, but despite everything, remember to keep moving forward on this journey. You can do this, and you can come out of this painful situation a much happier and healthier person.

CPSIA information can be obtained
at www.ICGtesting.com
Printed in the USA
LVHW010419130121
676360LV00006B/367